'There is a subtle but profound shift at work in *Why Christianity is Probably True*, a shift from the cocky certainty of far too many Western apologists who are given not only to arguments and reasons, but to brash insults of anyone who thinks their reasons might fall short of full proof. This book shifts the argument about God and about Jesus from the word "certain" to the word "probable," and the word "probable" takes just the sort of stance that can be given an ear in our world: a humble, generous, and kind stance that says "let's reason about this together, but give us believers a chance, will you please?" I have known many brilliant Christians over the years, but the ones who make the faith most credible (and probable), like Brian Harris, wear their learning lightly and show their faith in their life. One more time, please, give it a chance.'

Scot McKnight, Professor of New Testament, Northern Seminary

'Brian Harris takes the reader on a voyage that sets sail into the teeth of the secular seas in our conflicted world, identifying the jagged reefs that threaten Christianity as "intellectually vacuous, morally suspect, and experientially empty." With refreshing transparency, lucid argument, and winsome literary style, he navigates the sojourner to the shore.'

D   Religion and
Profi   n University

'In *Why Christianity is Pr...* ...resses many twenty-first century questions and concepts that challenge the authenticity, relevance and benevolence of the Christian faith. He does so thoughtfully, respectfully and carefully, with logical argument and reasoned conviction, without dodging genuine difficulties that the world at large has with the claims of Christianity, and without pompous dogma, but always peppered with tongue-in-cheek humour. Brian listens; he converses; he discusses facts and evidence; he invites. This book is engaging and accessible no matter which side of the Jesus debate one is on, a book that encourages reflection.'

Carolyn Tan, Adjunct Lecturer, Vose Seminary, Western Australia

'This is the Apologetic book I wish I had written! It's not argumentative, but in a helpful and pithy way explores the three key areas of any worldview: intellectually viable, morally good, experientially satisfying. Brian shows that the Christian worldview more than satisfies those three worldview longings. On such systematic consistency one has a strong foundation for personal faith.

'*Why Christianity is Probably True* is a guide for those who understand that Apologetics is about probability not certainty. It should be on any good Apologetic bookshelf.'

Ross Clifford, Principal, Morling Theological College

'Not only does Brian tackle some of the more pressing claims facing the Christian faith in the 21st Century, he does it with characteristic clarity and – perhaps more importantly – a disarming and affable demeanour that invites his readers to engage. Far from the antagonist and reactive approach of so many in this genre, Harris' writing is akin to someone inviting you into their home, listening to your concerns and then gently but articulately helping you to see through the haze, towards the powerful truth of the timeless Christian message.'

Jon Bergmann, Co-founder, Centre for Faith and
Life and CEO and Founder, Hatch Learning & Development

'When I pick up one of Brian Harris' books, I know the pages will reflect his exceptional capacity to engage both head and heart without one diminishing the other. His engagement in contemporary conversations is always inviting and never self-justifying. Perhaps the most remarkable accomplishment of this book lies in two quietly compelling invitations. To those whose starting premise is "There's probably no God", an invitation to recognize all that human society generally considers good, finds its roots in Christian faith at its best. And to those inclined towards the "There probably is a God" position, an encouragement to resist the stilling of the often marginal voices that can describe how Christianity will continue to be a force for good in human history.'

Karen Siggins, Lead Pastor, Lesmurdie Baptist Church

'True to its title, *Why Christianity is Probably True* encourages us to live with questions and doubts. However, the heartbeat of this book is gospel – good news. Every page is underpinned by personal faith founded on intellectual enquiry and life experience, providing an honest, orderly and gently persuasive examination of the claims of Christianity.

'The book's strength lies in its easy-to-read, conversational style which is used successfully to discuss a range of objections to Christian faith. As each question is examined, the reader benefits from interjections on related issues which offer important and profound insights. For example, we encounter critical advice about how to read the Bible, how to interpret history, how to recognize a Christ-like church and how to hold in tension the main tenets of Christian faith.

'In a way which is relevant to Christian believers as well as enquirers, this book reiterates the gospel invitation: read the Bible, encounter Christ for yourself, live a life of faith.'

Dr Debra Reid, Director of Undergraduate Studies and Tutor in
Old Testament, Spurgeon's College, London

Why Christianity is Probably True

Building the Case for a Reasoned, Moral and Relevant Faith

Brian Harris

Paternoster:
thinking faith

First published 2020 by Paternoster
Paternoster is an imprint of Authentic Media Ltd
PO Box 6326, Bletchley, Milton Keynes MK1 9GG.
authenticmedia.co.uk

British Library Cataloguing in Publication Data
A catalogue record for this book is available from the British Library

ISBN 978-1-78893-106-9
978-1-78893-107-6 (e-book)

Cover design by Arnel Gregorio arrowdesigns01@gmail.com
Printed and bound in Great Britain by Bell and Bain, Glasgow

This book is dedicated to the staff and students of Vose Seminary, with gratitude for enriching relationships, stretching discussions and genuine kindness.

Contents

Foreword

We live at a time when the spirit of anti-intellectualism, relativism, individualism, religious pluralism, and many other -isms and schisms of postmodernity dominate and influence our society. Living in such a society raises several questions on the legitimacy, validity and uniqueness of the Christian faith, especially when there are so many other religious and secular worldviews that are readily available to people. Over the years, I have encountered and answered thousands of apologetic questions in contexts such as universities, colleges, seminaries, organizations, churches and the marketplace. Reflecting on my apologetics ministry, I can safely say that most of these questions are based on the intellectual integrity, moral credibility and experiential relevance of the Christian faith.

Some people contend that the Christian gospel is a form of 'foolishness' to the world (1 Corinthians 1:18) and that Paul stayed clear of persuasive words of human wisdom (1 Corinthians 2:4). Therefore, we should not give in to the worldly wisdom of reason, logic or rationality, but focus on the spiritual aspects of the Christian faith. However, what we need to realize is that we live in a complex world and people are persuaded for many reasons. For some people, intellectual objections act as a serious and genuine barrier to the Christian faith. Some examples are the existence of God, the reliability of the Bible, the concept of the Holy Trinity, the resurrection of Christ, or any supernatural event in the Bible. These intellectual objections must be addressed sensitively and appropriately.

Moreover, once an atheist friend of mine quipped, 'Can anything good come out of religion?' She was reacting to the centuries of violence and bloodshed done in the name of God. When I look at the way the Christian faith was and is currently being abused and exploited for power, pleasure, and monetary or personal gains, it does make the practice of evangelism or apologetics extremely difficult. However, we must not confuse the followers of Christ with Christ himself or, for that matter, we must not confuse the followers of a worldview with the worldview itself. I am sure we can come up with several examples of individuals in each religious or secular worldview who are an embarrassment to it. That is why I always encourage my students to primarily critique the worldview and not its followers. Additionally, there are some ethical concerns, such as abortion, sexuality, race and gender issues, that still pose a problem for the moral credibility of the Christian faith.

Furthermore, in our postmodern individualistic society, we must not be surprised if someone raises the question, 'If I become a Christian, what's in it for me?' Some people might be convinced that the spiritual 'justification by faith' aspect of salvation has experiential relevance, but others might need more tangible evidence for it. Why are miracles not so common any more? Is faith a matter of belief, or can I actually experience God? Why does God often seem so distant? Also, I have come across people who have left their Christian faith because what they believed did not match their experience or what they are seeing happening in the world. They cannot reconcile a good, loving God with the evil taking place around the globe or in their immediate neighbourhood. Although questions on evil, pain and suffering are as old as humanity, they still dominate our apologetics today, and they need some serious and careful attention.

Now, the biggest strength of this book is that it tackles these issues head-on because these three aspects (intellectual integrity, moral credibility and experiential relevance), although termed slightly differently, serve as the three main parts of this book. I found the threefold substructure of each part beneficial and systematic. The first section carefully summarizes the issue by raising several objections to the Christian faith, the second section responds to these objections, and the third section summarizes the response and asks the reader to evaluate the evidence presented. The introductory section on probability and why we should not always expect absolute certainty was beneficial to the arguments of the three sections. I appreciate the logical progression of the argument in all three 'But Have You Considered?' chapters. I particularly commend the case for 'orthopathy' in apologetics. In postmodern apologetics, the role of feelings, empathy, emotions and passion must be considered in order to be effective. Orthopathy, along with orthodoxy and orthopraxy, can make the Christian faith more relatable and plausible. I also appreciate the fact that the book does not tell people why they are wrong about Christianity or what they should rather believe, but it carefully and respectfully presents the evidence and a case for the Christian faith, and asks the reader to be the judge and weigh it carefully.

It must be noted that the questions raised in this book are not really new as they have been in existence for several centuries. However, the way in which Brian explores and addresses them is refreshing and thought-provoking as he genuinely seeks to attend to the contemporary context. Several common misunderstandings of the Christian faith are carefully investigated and appropriately defended. With various illustrations, personal anecdotes and questions to reflect on, he provides a clear, coherent and sound articulation of the Christian faith. Unlike some apologetics texts where one has to read and reread a passage several times to understand the author's argument or point, the prose in this book is remarkably conversational and comprehensible for both academic and non-academic audiences. Moreover, the content is robust, coherent and invitational.

For both believers and non-believers, I hope and pray that this book will be a blessing as it demonstrates the intellectual integrity, moral credibility and experiential relevance of the Christian faith. I am not sure about other teachers of apologetics who are currently reading this foreword, but I am adding this book to my essential reading list for my unit on apologetics. I praise God for Brian's gifts of Christian leadership and teaching ministry, and I highly commend Brian for producing this timely and helpful resource.

Seidel Abel Boanerges
Lecturer in Christian Mission and Theology
Spurgeon's College, London

Preface

Why this book?

Because I think it is needed. I'm exasperated by the lazy but growing assumption that the Christian faith lacks intellectual, moral and experiential credibility. A serious look at the evidence suggests that the exact opposite is true.

Not that I am about to try to 'prove' to you that Christianity is true. Absolute proof is impossible in this life, and when promised, usually turns out to be misguided. Beware of those who acknowledge no doubt, either in their belief or in their lack of it. In reality there are many tough and challenging questions to be faced, whether you are a Christian believer, a believer in another faith, an agnostic or an atheist.

This book explores many of these questions. It doesn't offer easy solve-everything answers, but in weighing the evidence it does conclude that Christianity is probably true.

I'm sorry if 'probably' doesn't do it for you. 'I need more certainty than that,' I hear you say. Truth to tell, probably is where we should come out. After all, those who follow Jesus are called to a life of faith, and you don't need faith if everything is certain. What's more, in my experience, probably usually comes off. And when it comes to the Christian faith, I'm quietly confident that this won't be the exception . . .

I hope you enjoy reading the book as much as I have enjoyed writing it. It has been made so much easier by a supportive setting. My wife Rosemary is unfailing in her enthusiasm for my writing projects.

The staff and students at Vose Seminary (where I have the privilege of serving as Principal) provide an idyllic setting for my work. A more thoughtful, intelligent, good-hearted and hard-working community would be hard to find. I am indebted to them and, as partial payment, dedicate this book to them. They will probably read it and may well take pleasure in doing so. Special thanks to Dr Graeme Cross, our Academic Dean, who read the first draft and provided genuinely helpful feedback.

Brian Harris
Vose Seminary
Perth, Australia

1

Introduction: About Probability

Perhaps you have come across the bus campaign run by the New Atheists. The little slogan blazoned across the exterior of many buses runs 'There's probably no God. Now stop worrying and enjoy your life.' It's an interesting claim followed by a rather bossy but no doubt well-intentioned instruction. It doesn't say there is no God, but intentionally opts for the P word – *probably*. It then suggests an intriguing implication – that God's likely non-existence should release us from worry and enable us to enjoy life. It's an interesting perspective, all softened by that suggestive word 'probably'.

Actually, for most of human history the vast majority of people have assumed that God does exist. Large numbers have been pretty emphatic about it and have never given atheism even a passing nod. But others have acknowledged moments of doubt and would have said more modestly, 'God probably exists.'

Probably . . . it's about where the weight of evidence points. It's not about a single indisputable piece of proof (God will be at the local supermarket today, so visit the store before 5 p.m. and have all doubt erased), but the accumulation of many pieces of evidence, stacked up and considered. And as we consider them, we watch the balance of the scale tilt first in one direction, then another. Because we can never be certain we have found every possible piece of evidence, we can't be sure that the direction of the tilt will never change. But as with political elections, as more and more results are announced, at some point we feel confident that we can announce a verdict. At the early stages we proclaim it in the language of probability. Later we become more definite.

The assertion of this book is simple. If you seriously weigh the available evidence, you are likely to conclude both that God probably exists and that the Christian understanding of God is likely to be so close to accurate that the difference isn't worth quibbling about.

Now in spite of the laid-back tone, this is a bold claim. Can it be backed up? Yes it can, and I will do so in the pages that follow. While I can't be certain, I'm quietly confident that if you read this book to the end you too will say, 'So that's why Christianity is probably true', and I'm hopeful that you will say this regardless of your starting point (and perhaps right now you are thinking, 'That's hardly probable').

So what's the evidence?

I'd like to consider it in three broad categories. The evidence of reason, the evidence of history and the evidence of experience.

I've chosen these fairly deliberately, and done so in response to claims that are often made in an attempt to discredit the Christian faith, without needing to seriously engage with it or its claims. These are that it is intellectually vacuous, morally suspect and experientially empty. The book is divided into three sections, and each will consider one of these claims.

The first section, 'But Faith is Intellectually Vacuous' is divided into three chapters: 'So Here's the Problem', followed by 'But Have You Considered?', and then there is an invitation, 'Let's Weigh This Up'.

The remaining two sections follow the same format, with section B centred on the statement 'But Faith is Morally Suspect' and section C, 'But Faith is Experientially Empty'.

You may well have heard the claim, 'Absence of evidence is evidence of absence', often made on the unverified assumption that there is no serious evidence to point to the likely veracity of the Christian faith. Actually, potential evidence is everywhere. It depends on whether we have the eyes to spot it and the intellectual rigour to carefully consider it.

Not that this book will attempt to make faith redundant. It could be claimed that the opposite of faith is not doubt but certainty, for where there is certainty, faith is not needed. If it is certainty you need, this book won't provide it. And that's as it should be, because reasonable steps of faith characterize all human life. As you know, you can't be certain you won't be hit by a bus on your next venture into town (it could even be one with the slogan 'There's probably no God'), but it's unlikely to stop you making the trip.

I hope that what you read makes the step of faith needed attainable – not a huge and blind leap in the dark, but a logical next step in a journey that points in a solid and reputable direction. Actually, it could be more than just solid and reputable. It could be life-changing. For if God probably exists, there is every reason to stop worrying and to get on and enjoy your life – and to do so with far greater purpose, confidence and hopefulness.

Section A

But Faith is Intellectually Vacuous

2

So Here's the Problem: Faith is Intellectually Vacuous

For most of human history, belief in the existence of God has been hardwired into our existence. Almost every society has had some form of religious faith, the most significant difference usually being whether the people believed in one god or several. While many individuals have had what can be called a **practical atheism** (the existence or otherwise of a god or gods making no difference to the way they actually lived their lives), few have embraced an **intellectual atheism**. In other words, while many people have lived as though God does not exist, if you asked them if they believed in the existence of God, they would almost always have answered 'yes'. We could say that belief in God has been the overwhelming default drive for the vast majority of the human race in almost every society and at almost every time in history.

But that's starting to change.

True, there is some debate as to whether atheism is growing. Globally it seems to be struggling, a recent study claiming that whereas 4.5% of the world's population could be classified as atheist in 1970, that number had dropped to 2% in 2010 and is predicted to be a mere 1.8% by 2020.[1] The main cause of the decline has been the demise of once officially atheist states, such as those in Eastern Europe, where the arrival of religious freedom has led to dramatic increases in those professing a religious faith, most commonly of the Christian or Muslim variety. However, that picture changes very quickly when you explore the terrain in countries that were once a bastion of the Christian faith. A recent report in *National Geographic* noted that Australia, France, the Netherlands, New Zealand and the United Kingdom all already have, or in the near future are likely to have, a majority secular population who claim no religious faith.[2] This is especially true of the younger sector of the population, which would suggest that any reversal of this trend in these countries in the foreseeable future is unlikely.

What has caused the shift?

Though no single factor will be adequate on its own, we should note the rise of what is commonly called the 'New Atheism', which has been especially influential in the countries cited by *National Geographic*, as well as in the USA and Canada. Following the appalling Islamist terrorist attack on the World Trade Center in New York on 11 September 2001, the so-called 'Four Horsemen of the New Atheism' (Richard Dawkins, Sam Harris, Daniel Dennett and the late Christopher Hitchens) galloped into public consciousness with a series of popular books and public presentations proclaiming the end of religion. The most popular of these has been Richard Dawkins' book *The God Delusion*, which has sold well over 3 million copies.[3]

In trying to understand why atheism has found a fresh and new appeal in much of the so-called western world, it helps to look at the claims made in *The God Delusion*.

Dawkins' central argument is that the existence of God is extremely improbable because God would require a designer. While people of faith often claim that a world that shows evidence of design must have a designer, they usually don't address the obviously related question of who designed God. Indeed, Dawkins argues that introducing the idea of God as an explanation for reality complicates rather than clarifies the issues. Furthermore, Dawkins argues that while science is evidence-based, religion relies upon ignorance, fear and superstition. Science has now reached the point where we can explain the existence of the universe without having to resort to the so-called **God hypothesis**, which usually sees God as a prop used to fill in the blanks of what we were otherwise unable to explain (if you can't explain it, attribute it to God). The God hypothesis is thus now tired and unnecessary, and its explanatory power is in rapid retreat.

But Dawkins' critique goes further than this. Not content to merely settle for the likely non-existence of God (so sad, too bad), Dawkins presses further and argues that this is all for the good. Strongly arguing against the commonly held notion that people require religion to guide them along loving and moral paths, he alleges that the source of Christian morality, the Bible, is itself immoral – and he selects some of the more extreme biblical passages to justify his oft-quoted claim that: 'The God of the Old Testament is arguably the most unpleasant character in all fiction: jealous and proud of it; a petty, unjust, unforgiving control-freak; a vindictive, bloodthirsty ethnic cleanser; a misogynistic, racist, infanticidal, genocidal, filicidal, pestilential, megalomaniacal, sadomasochistic, capriciously malevolent bully.'[4] Now while that quote does little more than establish that Dawkins has an impressive vocabulary and a love of hyperbole, it has had its impact. Those who previously assumed that religion was a force for good in the world have started to seriously question this premise. Many have found this challenge unsettling; for some it is so unsettling that they have abandoned prior faith commitments.

Though the track record of those countries that have committed to an officially atheistic stance is deeply discouraging (think Russia under Stalin), the New Atheists are hopeful that an embrace of atheism will lead us to moral maturity. They hope that if we see reality for what it is, and live with our finitude in mind, it might herald a kinder, gentler and more tolerant future, far removed from the bigotry that religion so often propels us towards.

Not that these objections of Dawkins represent a complete list of reasons to question faith.[5] In no particular order we can note that:

- Some people find the plethora of religious options bewildering and self-defeating (as different religions are often mutually contradictory, they can't possibly all be true; indeed, perhaps they are all equally untrue).

- The religious writings that support the world's major religions are also seen as a stumbling block. The Bible's description of a six-day creation (followed by a rest day) is dismissed as impossible, its record of a global flood that destroyed everything bar those creatures protected by Noah in his ark is rejected as bizarre, while the claim that Jesus rose from the dead is understood, at best, as wishful thinking.

- For others, the fundamental injustice of the universe strikes a decisive death blow to any claim that a loving God upholds the world.

- Yet others argue that if God intends to dispatch billions to hell, Hitler starts to look like St Francis in comparison.

In a twitter age, where arguments are seldom developed in depth, or ideas carefully scrutinized, the sheer sensationalism of these claims is appealing to many. Whereas atheism was once the domain of a small sector of the academic elite, it is possible that its new-found popularity (in certain parts of the globe) will see that change, with atheism now the default position of the masses – not because of its intellectual rigour, but because it is being marketed with effective slogans and sweepingly dismissive claims.

In the following chapters we will see if some of these attempts to discredit faith are really as strong as they might seem on the surface.

3

But Have You Considered? Some Logical Reasons to Believe

In the previous chapter we quickly surveyed some key objections to religious faith. This follows most people's current experience, where they are first told *why* they can't believe, with faith dismissed as a naive or credulous relic from a distant past. Rather than dismiss arguments for belief as primitive superstitions best suited to a world that no longer exists, let's give them a fair hearing.

The sensible place to start is to look at some pointers towards the existence of God. We'll begin by looking at the case for theism and follow it by then exploring the argument for Christian theism.

The case for theism

Thomas Aquinas and the 'necessary first being' argument

Theism claims that there is a God who is the creator of the universe. It does not go much further than that. This God could be the one worshipped in Judaism, Christianity, Islam, Hinduism (for theism does not insist that there can only be one God) and potentially a host of other faiths besides. While not much content is attached to this belief, it stands in stark contrast to its opposite, atheism, which as the term suggests is a denial of theism, thus a[as in anti]-theism.

The first argument for theism is that of creation, or the indisputable fact that the world exists. In Psalm 19:1 the psalmist writes,

'The heavens declare the glory of God'. For most of human history, this has been a largely uncontested insight. When faced with the wonder of creation, it has been usual to default to the position of 'Only God could have made this . . . it cannot possibly be the result of random chance'. Don't take this too lightly. When we stand at the top of a mountain and look out at spectacular scenery below, or when we find refreshment and renewal as we watch the ocean's waves roll in, something inside us instinctively reaches out in thanksgiving. We are grateful for what we see, and sense that we should be thanking someone – someone who must have been there before us to get this all going. Of course this doesn't prove the existence of God, but it is an interesting quirk inside us. It is as though we have been made to worship. It seems reasonable to ask why – and possibly the answer is that we feel a need to worship because there is someone to worship.

Thomas Aquinas (1225–74) gave this intuitive conviction some words in his outline of five ways to prove God exists. For those into nuance, each of the five ways is indeed subtly different from the others, but in principle they boil down to one point, arguably made most forcibly in his third way, the argument from possibility and necessity (the *reductio* argument). This third point is helpfully summarized into a series of logical steps by Theodore Gracyk:[1]

1. We find in nature things that are possible to be and not to be, that come into being and go out of being, i.e. contingent beings.
2. Assume that every being is a contingent being.
3. For each contingent being, there is a time it does not exist.
4. Therefore it is impossible for these always to exist.
5. Therefore there could have been a time when no things existed.
6. Therefore at that time there would have been nothing to bring the currently existing contingent beings into existence.
7. Therefore, nothing would be in existence now.
8. We have reached an absurd result from assuming that every being is a contingent being.
9. Therefore not every being is a contingent being.

10. Therefore some being exists of its own necessity, and does not receive its existence from another being, but rather causes them. This all men speak of as God.

Put differently, and at the risk of oversimplifying, nothing comes from nothing, so the fact that there is something indicates that there must be a pre-existent eternal something (or someone), whom we call 'God'. As Timothy Keller puts it: 'because all natural beings have a cause, there must be some supernatural entity that exists without a cause from which all has come.'[2]

The fact that the 'something' that has come into existence is so complex and awe-inspiring says much about the originator of it all, presupposing that it is more logical to assume that the direction of movement is from the complex to the simple (rather than the simple to the complex), for we usually create things that are simpler than ourselves. In other words, if the world is this sophisticated, how much more sophisticated must God be.

Note that this argument not only provides a reason to believe in God but also answers the question 'So who created God?' The answer is that God is uncreated – the eternally pre-existent being. Following Aquinas's argument as summarized above, this is an appropriate conclusion, for without a pre-existent being, nothing could exist. As things do exist, there must be a pre-existent first cause. Put differently, God simply is, and nothing really makes sense unless God is.

The argument can be escalated. We live on a Goldilocks planet – one that so nearly would not have been able to permit life, but in the end appears to have been fine-tuned so that everything was 'just right' for life to exist on this planet.[3] We so nearly weren't. Is this luck, or design? Add to this the sheer beauty of our planet. It is not just that somehow life has managed to eke its way into being, but that we live in a breathtakingly beautiful world – and strangely, humans are able to spot beauty everywhere. Even the desert intrigues and fascinates us, which from an evolutionary perspective is puzzling, for the inhospitality of its terrain should make us wary and want to stay away, instead of bringing out the poet and artist inside us.

Again we could put this differently. Even if somehow matter simply was (there being something without any first cause for that something), the likelihood of that matter taking the form of something that appeared to be designed is remote. This understates the case. The difficulty of arriving at a planet as majestic, yet as delicately balanced, as our own should not be downplayed. Those not convinced by the argument often dismissively reply that we are forgetting that though the statistical odds against arriving at a planet like our own are staggering, if these odds are set against a backdrop of infinite time and an infinite number of opportunities (and no one to know if it didn't come off), in the end the arrival of our planet was inevitable, as the laws of science and nature simply ticked away as one failed attempt followed billions and billions and billions of other attempts until one day – *voilà* – the conditions were exactly right, and planet earth got under way.

Hmm, perhaps, except note that even this explanation assumes a pre-existent something: the laws of science. Where did they come from? Or should we understand the laws of science to be God – the pre-existent force driving all that could be, uncreated but creative in their being?

It comes down to the most basic of dilemmas. We are . . . and since Descartes' groundbreaking insight 'I think, therefore I am', we have had no serious reason to doubt our existence, for we are conscious of it. While non-existence would be non-problematic and require no explanation (which is just as well, as there would be no one to make it), existence demands explanation, especially conscious existence. In other words, it is not just that I am – I *know* that I am, and I know that I am not you. About 99% of the human body is composed of six key elements: oxygen, hydrogen, carbon, nitrogen, calcium and phosphorus, a range of other elements making up the remaining 1%. Our chemical composition, however, in no way provides an explanation for our animation – or to express it loosely, it does not explain why we are conscious carbon (or conscious hydrogen, oxygen, nitrogen and so on). We are more than matter; we are conscious matter. The existence of conscious life demands an explanation.

While you can categorize the answers given to the dilemma of our existence in a variety of ways, in the end they essentially boil down to two: random chance, or intentional creation by a pre-existent force (almost always named God). Ultimately you must decide which of these two has greater explanatory power and which seems to accord most closely with the facts as we are currently able to establish them.

A sense of 'ought': our moral make-up

If the first key argument for theism is existence (which must be explained by an uncreated first mover – God), the second is that we exist in a moral universe, or in a universe where there is a universal moral standard. Now, true, not all morality is universally agreed. There are those who believe it is not an affront to serve instant coffee, and there are a multitude of dubious fashion, music and culinary choices that leave many unbothered. But much morality is instinctively grasped, even by those who argue that all morality is relative.

So, for example, if you are minding your own business while strolling down the road, and someone walks up to you and punches you on the nose, after yelping in pain you would almost certainly think 'That's not right. It's just not fair' – or possibly some similar sentiment in stronger terms. But why is it not fair or right? Presupposing that neither you nor your kin had previously done any harm to the punch-thrower, nearly everyone would agree that the action was wrong. This near universal moral standard (don't punch noses, don't kill, don't steal, don't harm) requires some explanation. Where does it come from? What is the origin of this sense of 'ought to' and 'ought not to'?

Theists usually argue that there can be a universal moral standard only if God exists, for where else is the source for morality? *If the world is essentially arbitrary and accidental, it takes a leap of faith to believe that it is also accidentally moral.*

Today we argue strongly that there are universal human rights, and attempt to punish dictators who for a period of time violated these rights simply because they had the power to do so. We do not buy into the 'might is right' argument, and are willing to hold people accountable for their actions, judging them against a set of largely agreed universal human rights. But why should every human person have inalienable rights? If we have simply evolved as a result of the survival of the fittest, surely the powerful should muscle out the weak, for how else could our race be confident that our best genes are propagated, or that its reproductive potential is safeguarded? As Timothy Keller expresses it: 'We evolved through the strong overcoming the weak, so there is nothing natural about the idea of human rights . . . human rights make more sense in a universe created by God. Without God, it is difficult to explain why or how they exist.'[4]

Some argue that morality has evolved because it serves an evolutionary function and aids the survival of our species. Richard Dawkins, for example, has proposed a 'selfish gene' which, while it outwardly appears to promote altruism, in reality leads to circumstances where our own advancement is more probable.[5] As such, although it often appears to be moral behaviour we are engaged in, a more realistic observer would note that the underlying motivation is self-interest. While this is perhaps true of much human behaviour where we cooperate helpfully with others, looking for what we often call 'win-win' solutions, there are many scenarios where this is an inadequate explanation. We often look out for the interests of the poor and vulnerable, and consider it our duty to do so. From an evolutionary perspective, that which is weak and vulnerable is supposed to disappear in the relentless survival of the fittest. Yet we consider ourselves to be at our finest when we transcend narrow self-interest and act altruistically on behalf of those who are struggling. And why do we feel we are ultimately accountable for our actions if there is no one to account to?

It is a fact that with the advent of Christianity altruism was more readily valued. Prior to Jesus, the wisdom of the parable of the Good Samaritan was not considered obvious. The Jewish audience who first heard Jesus tell this story would have readily agreed with the argument if it weren't for Jesus provocatively insisting that the doer of the good deed was a Samaritan. Doing good within your own family or national circle was conventional wisdom; looking out for the interests of the foreigner and the enemy was not. Part of the argument for the probable truth of Christianity is that it takes basic human impulses, such as our sense of moral obligation, and elevates them to new levels, opening up an ethical framework which would otherwise have proved elusive.

These arguments are not decisive on their own, but, rather than reach a conclusion now, put them in the balancing scales to be weighed up with some additional evidence, to which we now turn. It will help us to assess not just the case for theism but for Christian theism.

What should we make of the Bible?

The role of the Bible in building or diminishing the case for Christianity is important. While arguments for theism establish that belief in a god or gods is reasonable, at some point we have to give content to the character and nature of the god believed in. Although a certain amount can be ascertained from nature (what kind of god would have to exist if the world as we know it reflects this god's ingenuity?), a lot remains uncertain. After all, if you look at a sunset at the end of a tranquil and glorious day, you will probably praise 'this good God', but if your examination takes place in the aftermath of a tsunami, your conclusions may be very different. How can we draw solid conclusions about the character of God if creation is our only guide?

This is why theologians usually insist that we should study two books: the 'book' of nature and the Bible. From the book of nature we learn much about that which falls into the category of **general revelation** (those things which can be discerned by any fair and open-minded individual on the basis of evidence readily available to most human beings), while we are dependent on the Bible to show us those things which we would otherwise never be sure of bar God's revelation of them in the Bible – what we can call **special revelation**. The Bible is seen as a key (perhaps the key) source of special revelation because here God self-introduces via a series of 'God turned up' events that reveal the plans and purposes of God for the world.

Christians maintain that these events were faithfully recorded by the various biblical authors and led ultimately to the Bible as we have it today. In short, minus the Bible, it is difficult to give much more than the most elementary commentary on the personality or purposes of the god (or gods) that theism encourages us to believe in.

In theory, then, it is not hard to understand why a book like the Bible is necessary if we are going to develop an understanding of God that is not built on the at best tentative (and sometimes conflicting) observations gained from the book of nature.

If the role of the Bible is to give clarity and certainty as to the character, plans and purposes of God, is it a credible witness?

It is here that the argument gets interesting, for the Bible is clearly a remarkable book. Perhaps it is not too much of a stretch to suggest that it is a miraculous book.

Consider its composition. It was written over a period of approximately sixteen hundred years by about forty different authors, being completed around nineteen hundred years ago. Let that sink in . . .

If you knew nothing about the Bible and were told 'I'd like you to read a book written by forty people over a period of sixteen hundred years and completed nineteen hundred years ago', what would your expectation be?

Be honest. While you might be a little intrigued, you'd be unlikely to approach it with bated breath. How would such a book hold together? We struggle to make sense of books written two hundred years ago by a single author. How could this multi-authored, far more ancient book be relevant? Would you expect themes like family life, or love, or justice, or the hundreds of other topics that are touched on to make much sense? Probably not. You are even less likely to think that it would have much contemporary relevance.

Yet, ancient text that it is, the Bible continues as a world bestseller. Why?

There is a very simple answer. People continue to find it relevant and helpful. Some make bolder claims, and say it is life-transforming – a sure guide for faith and life.

Any fair investigator of history will quickly tell you that the impact of the Bible has not been limited to its outworking in the lives of pious individuals. This book has literally shaped the world as we know it. True, other faiths have their own books for which special inspiration is claimed, but if we work with the simple criterion of which has had the greatest impact, it turns into a one-horse race. The Bible's impact has no near rival.[6]

You may be a sceptical reader. If so, I can hear you argue back, 'No one disputes the impact of the Bible. But that's the problem. Have you read the book? It is so bloodthirsty – at times barbaric. And people still hold it up as a moral guide. Perhaps it was a guide in a desperately dark and dreadful past, but mercifully we have made some progress, and the Bible's use-by date as a moral guide has long since dawned. We now operate with superior ethical insights which would be compromised if we allowed ourselves to be held ransom to the dictates of this dated text.' At that point you might even throw in a reference to one of the Bible's more gruesome passages – and there are a fair number of corpses scattered around its pages. Perhaps you would think that settles the debate, and be willing to dismiss the Bible as a quaint but clearly now obsolete relic.

I'd like to challenge you to a closer reading of the text. It is more penetrating in its analysis of life than you might currently imagine. And though some people make much of its more difficult passages, most of it reads easily and inspiringly. I read it every day, and find myself challenged afresh over and over again. You don't have to read it for long to realize that it is in a league of its own. Its world-shaping status was gained for good reason.

Remember, the Bible's most recent passages were written around nineteen hundred years ago, so it is as well to compare it with other texts from that era (or eras, for its writers spanned about sixteen centuries). If you do, you quickly discover its difference. In its own way, it is remarkably self-effacing. While other writings from antiquity are boastfully triumphalist, the Bible spends much of its time telling the story of the people of Israel, more often dwelling on their failures than their successes. The nuance in the text is astonishing. Its heroes have flaws; its villains have virtues. It recognizes the complexity of life.

It has several books which are best described as **wisdom literature**, and they host a fascinating internal discussion. There is the homely wisdom of the book of Proverbs – insightful, but you know it isn't always as simple as any one proverb suggests. Which is why there is the counter-argument found in Ecclesiastes, where the author dives into the existential angst of life: 'Everything is meaningless and then you die' is the superficial reading of his approach. Add to that the insights of Job and you find yourself quickly immersed in the question of innocent suffering. No trite answers are allowed. As you read the different books of wisdom, it is as though you are being given options. You initially find yourself being persuaded in one direction, but as you make your way through, you discover an 'on the other hand' starting to emerge. The honesty is breathtaking, and the complexity of life is readily acknowledged. You start to realize that colliding truths help us to dive into the depth of a matter, and that paradox is a gift to embrace. It is not too hard to understand why, even thousands of years after being written, this book remains the world's bestseller.

Naturally, as with most profound books, it helps to have a little guidance on how to best read it. In another book I have written, *The Big Picture: Building Blocks of a Christian World View*, I speak of the importance of having orienting passages to help us navigate the various themes found in the Bible, and I suggest fifteen passages to help in this regard.[7] The idea behind this is simple enough. Once we have deeply understood some of the key passages in the Bible, it helps us to understand other passages against the backdrop of its key concerns. When we do this, many things fall into place. Often the more bizarre accusations made against the Bible violate this principle, and haul passages out of their context and setting, making it sound as though the Bible supports the indefensible. A fair and balanced reading usually quietens such concerns.

So how does the Bible help us to journey towards belief? It is clearly a remarkable book, which has deeply impacted human history. It has changed the lives of multitudes. One of the claims that it makes is that God uses the Bible to speak to us deeply, Hebrews 4:12 stating: 'For the word of God is alive and active. Sharper than any double-edged sword, it penetrates even to dividing soul and spirit, joints and marrow; it judges the thoughts and attitudes of the heart.'

A challenge like this is not to be avoided. Why not read it for yourself and see if it makes any difference to you? The old saying goes that 'The proof of the pudding is in the eating', and even if your experience of the Bible might not convince multitudes of others, it is likely to convince *you* – and that seems to be a fair starting point.

Thus far I have made some fairly general, though valid, comments about the Bible. There are those who cite the Bible as one of the reasons they find it difficult to believe the Christian faith, so let's consider some of the specific objections raised.

The most common is that its content is simply non-credible. Accused of parading as history, it is dismissed as a collection of myths and fables which even the slightest intellect would quickly reject.

Much of this claim is linked to the first eleven chapters of the Bible, which give a brief account of world history prior to the formation of the Hebrew people. 'Brief' is the key descriptor here. Eleven chapters to cover all human history prior to the formation of a particular nation is more than an ambitious project; it is an impossible one. Very wisely, the Bible attempts this task with only the broadest of broad strokes.

Its thrust is not to establish historical credibility but to introduce key theological themes, such as creation, the fall of humanity, the stuttering and inadequate attempts of human beings to build a relationship with God and one another. Free yourself from the question 'But is this precisely as it happened?' and allow yourself to ask, 'What view of the world, God and humanity do these chapters give me?', and you might find yourself moving from dismissing these chapters as 'obviously untrue' to a verdict of 'pretty thought-provoking'.

Put slightly differently, if you find it reasonable to accept, for example, that Genesis chapters 1 to 3 are not primarily an attempt to explain *how* God made the world but *why* God made the world, you are likely to read them very differently. Indeed, you are probably starting to read them as they were intended to be read, which is a wise move.

This leads to a self-evidently sensible proposal, preceded by a statement. As a collection of sixty-six books written over a period of around sixteen hundred years, the Bible contains a variety of literary genres. To validly interpret the Bible, we should pay attention to the different genres and assess each biblical passage in the light of its genre. For example, if you read poetry as history, you will dismiss it as unreliable. Once you correctly classify it as poetry, the problem disappears. This is an entirely reasonable proposition, and if accepted, the majority of objections about the trustworthiness of the Bible's content simply evaporate. This comes as no surprise to serious scholars of the Bible, who for many years have paid close attention to the subject of hermeneutics, which is the theory and methodology of interpreting the Bible. When I listen to the accusations that many of the New Atheists make about the Bible, I sometimes wonder if they have heard of hermeneutics. The cavalier way in which many of them quote biblical passages outside their literary context makes it hard to seriously entertain the objection raised.

Let's explore three other doubts raised about the Bible.

First, is it essentially a bloodthirsty text, a relic of an era which saw might as right and myopically considered any means valid so long as it furthered the author's end? Second, given that this is such an ancient text and one that evolved in an essentially oral culture, can we be sure that the version we currently read bears close resemblance to what was originally written? Finally, the Bible talks about many miraculous events that are hard to believe; is it reasonable to believe in miracles?

Is the Bible a bloodthirsty text?

We have already noted that the genre of any text must be noted. For example, if the Bible describes a battle that takes place, it is in the first instance a description of a battle. It is not intended as an inspirational piece which we are to model and attempt to replicate in our life. Nor does the description of the battle necessarily denote God's approval of what takes place, even if God's name is attached to it. Do remember that the ancients attached God's name to everything. This was their way of affirming that God is always aware of what occurs in life and is ultimately the source of all life; therefore nothing, be it good or evil, can be seen outside the reality of the existence of God, without whom nothing would exist.

We can put this differently and say that we must differentiate between what the Bible describes and what it teaches. When something is explicitly taught, we must also decide if it is being taught for a particular context (for example, some of the food laws in the Bible made great sense in a desert climate in an age prior to refrigeration), or if the teaching is meant to be valid for all time. Usually it is best to look for the underlying principles that sit behind any particular instruction. While the specific instruction may not be universally valid, the underlying principles usually are.

An example of this is found in the story of Joseph, told in Genesis 37 – 50. One terrible thing after another happens to Joseph. He is sold into slavery by his brothers (and you thought your family had problems!) and is later thrown into jail after being falsely accused of attempted rape. An innocent man, for years he is forgotten and appears to be abandoned by God. But then his fortunes turn around, and in a very short space of time he becomes the second most powerful person in Egypt, second only to Pharaoh. Great good eventually comes from his life and suffering. Genesis 50:20 provides the dramatic summary. Joseph is speaking to his brothers who had him sold into slavery. They expect nothing but punishment from him, but instead he replies (and this is a paraphrase): 'Why would I punish you? What you intended for evil, God has worked out for good. God has used your evil to save the lives of many people.'

It is the reality of this assessment which we must note. Joseph never lauds his brothers' actions as good or worthy of duplication, but notes that despicable though they were, God has been able to bring good from them. This is how many passages in the Bible work. They describe desperately sad and broken situations – situations that the Bible never suggests are good – and then follow the often tangled web of circumstances to find how a loving God eventually finds a redemptive path forward, even in the most hopeless of circumstances.

To read every situation described in the Bible as having a 'thumbs up' from God is a misguided way of reading the text. This becomes especially clear when we read 1 Chronicles 22:6–10 and 28:1–3. I earlier mentioned the helpfulness of orienting passages when reading Scripture. In my book *The Big Picture*, I select these as some of them, and here is what I wrote about these verses:

> On more than one occasion I have been asked to defend the moral vision of the Bible, and particularly that of the Old Testament. The issue is the many corpses scattered across its pages. A quick reading could leave the impression that God is very one-sided, caring about the Israelites but having little time for anyone else. While the loss of Hebrew lives on the battlefields of the Bible is seen as tragic, Canaanite, Philistine and Egyptian carcasses don't really seem to matter.
>
> 1 Chronicles 22:6–10 and 28:1–3 give a clearer insight into the heart-beat of God. In these passages David explains that God had forbidden him to build the temple because the warfare with which he was associated excluded him from the project. For its time, this is radically counter-cultural, especially as ancient kings routinely built temples to thank their gods for military victories.
>
> These passages are fascinating. After all, David's many military victories are attributed to God's help. David would never have defeated the giant Goliath unless God had made it possible. Why does God now decline David's services as temple builder? We must conclude that whilst God agreed that the brokenness of David's time required tough military action, God was unwilling for warrior imagery to be associated with the temple. In short, God makes it clear that warfare is a tragic consequence of human evil, and that it will never have the last word. Isaiah 2:4 imagines a day when swords will be beaten into ploughshares, and spears into pruning hooks. This is what we should long for and work towards. Jesus

reminds us in Matthew 5:9 that it is peacemakers, not peace breakers, who are the children of God. When placed in the impossible situation of having to choose between bad and worse, it is true that warfare was sometimes seen as the lesser evil, but to imagine that it is therefore God's ideal is to ignore the witness of the temple David didn't build.[8]

Those who accuse the Bible of glorying in bloodshed, or being unconcerned about the fate of any but the Israelites, have not read the Bible with the complete text in mind. They have allowed themselves to become stuck on an individual troubling passage without allowing the overall weight of Scripture to move them forward. They are also not reading the Bible Christologically (that is, reading the whole of the Bible in the light of the life, teaching and resurrection of Jesus), which is another important hermeneutical principle that should be followed, and one of the significant differentiators between Christianity and Judaism.

Let me give you one more example.

I have heard people 'tut tut' in disgust and dismay when they hear Psalm 137:9. Speaking to the Babylonians it yells out, 'Happy are those who seize your infants and dash them against the rocks' (TNIV). At multiple levels this seems an ugly and alarming verse. It is about revenge, and even worse, taking revenge on the enemy's children rather than directly on the enemy. Those who have children know that often the most devastating way to attack someone is to attack them through their offspring, so this is assuredly one of the ugliest forms of revenge. Consequently, some have cited this verse as a reason to reject the Bible as a moral guide.

But why not dig a little deeper?

Psalm 137 originates from a specific and tragic historical context. The psalmist remembers sitting alongside the rivers of Babylon. Now these rivers, the Tigris and Euphrates, were the pride of Babylon and the reason that it was a fertile and viable country. But it was not Jewish territory, so what was the author doing there?

In all probability the writer had been taken into Babylonian captivity after the destruction of Judah, Jerusalem and its temple by the

Babylonians, which took place around 586 BCE. It was perhaps the most devastating time in the history of the Hebrew people. Their Northern Kingdom had been conquered by the Assyrians in 722 BCE, and now the remainder of their territory had been taken from them. They were traumatized exiles in a foreign country – and traumatized they would certainly have been.

Warfare in the ancient world was always brutal, and the Babylonians were no exception to this rule. Thousands of women would have been raped, children and the elderly would have been slaughtered, farms burnt to the ground, and the fit and healthy taken as slaves to serve their overlords in Babylon. It is probably while on the journey to this foreign land that this party of captives is forced to stop for a period of rest and recovery. While there, one of their Babylonian guards has the bright idea of suggesting a bit of a sing-a-long. Having heard about 'the songs of Zion' he urges the captives to sing one of them. In verse 3 of Psalm 137 the writer remembers the incident and recoils. It is a bridge too far. The prisoners resist. Hanging up the harps that were part of the spoil of conquest, they refuse to sing.

While recounting the incident, the writer finds himself (probably 'himself', though perhaps herself) weeping uncontrollably (v. 1). It has all been too much . . . far, far too much. Memories of burnt flesh, slaughtered people and children's terrified cries (perhaps his own child's terrified cries) come flooding back. The Jerusalem that once was springs back to mind. Deep within, the writer finds a desperate longing welling up. How could he ever have taken those earlier days in Jerusalem for granted? He makes a vow: if he ever forgets Jerusalem or adapts to the surrounding culture of his imprisonment, he asks that his tongue would stick to the roof of his mouth (v. 6). He knows that the land now lost, and the season now past, would always represent his highest joy, and there was no going back there.

It's haunting stuff – poetry at its best.

And then a rage settles upon the author. The flashbacks to the terrible time of destruction won't stop. He remembers how the Edomites – estranged close relatives to the Jews – had laughed and mocked when they saw what the Babylonians were doing (v. 7). If only it had stopped at their laughing . . . but it hadn't. They had urged the Babylonians on in the slaughter of Jewish babies and children. A furious anger overwhelms him. He can't help himself . . . the words rush out . . . he rants against his enemies the Edomites and Babylonians with a hatred so intense that you can feel it: 'Happy are those who seize your infants and dash them against the rocks,' he yells (v. 9).

Two and a half thousand years later, in our tidy homes and impressive lounges, we read the psalm again, and saturated in luxury as we are, we sit in judgement on it.

'Not very nice to ask God to kill other people's children,' we say. 'Fancy that being in the Bible.'

And so we miss the point. This is not a 'business as usual' psalm. It is written in a place of torment and personal agony. It is from the land of deepest regret and overwhelming sorrow – the place where everything has been lost. And the lament is addressed to God, for the psalmist knows one thing for sure: when everything in life is lost, there is only one place you can turn. And so he screams out his pain to God . . . And all those who have suffered and are suffering deeply read his cry and take heart, for they know they are not alone. If they read the psalm wisely and well, they take their pain and sorrow, and like the psalmist of old they place it in the hands of God. No, they don't rush out and kill babies and children, but they do know that the God of all the earth can be trusted with our deepest hurts and heartbreaks. And so this psalm continues to speak powerfully and transformingly to us.

This is no toxic text. It helps us to deal with our deepest pains. Thousands of years before the psychological importance of catharsis was noted, the Bible opens a window on the importance of lament. It models a way for us to find release from our deepest sorrows.

In summary, when we read the Bible as a whole, and especially when we read it in the light of the story of Jesus, the moral objections to the text quickly fade. Instead we are caught up with the wonder of the text. But instead of my simply telling you that this is an astonishing and life-transforming book, can I repeat my suggestion that you actually read it – and that you do so with an open mind. That way you can discover for yourself if this book deserves its status as the most read book in all of human history. Certainly its continued existence and wide distribution is itself worthy of comment, and perhaps suggests that there is another hand behind its story – perhaps even the hand of God.

Can we be sure that the text we read today bears a reasonable resemblance to the text originally written?

Some people worry that the Bible we read today does not represent the text that was originally written. They also wonder if the process of deciding what to include in the Bible involved illegitimate interference with the historical documents, allowing the church to include in the Bible those passages that suited its message and to exclude those that might have been more troublesome. Many have read Dan Brown's sensational *The Da Vinci Code*, and wonder if there may be suppressed but credible stories of Jesus that suggest he might have been married and had children and . . . well, the list goes on and on. They have forgotten that while appealing to conspiracy theorists, Brown's book is a novel – a work of fiction.[9]

Now it is true that there are accounts of Jesus that do not make it into the pages of the Bible. Most were written in the second century or later (in other words, long after the writing of the gospels as found in the Bible), and contain material that is hard to believe – and which the church has not suggested we should believe. Essentially they prove that Jesus was an enormously important person, worth writing about, and that as time went by there was more and more speculation about his life.

How then can we be sure that the four biographies of Jesus which we find in the Bible (Matthew, Mark, Luke and John) are trustworthy, and not carefully edited works of historical fiction written to further the agenda of the fledgling church?

Let's face the problem square on. There are no surviving original manuscripts of the New Testament, and nor, for that matter, of any of the four gospels. Sceptics might complain, 'OK, so all we have are copies of copies of copies. Sounds convincing!'

The first thing to note is that this statement is true of all material we have from the ancient world.

Ask how we can be sure that Cleopatra or Julius Caesar or a host of other historical figures from the ancient world existed, and the answer comes back, 'From evidence that is fragmentary and long removed from the people and events described'. In fact, excluding the Bible, the best documentary evidence we have for any event in the ancient world is Homer's *Iliad*, an epic poem from ancient Greece set during the Trojan War and telling of the quarrel between King Agamemnon and Achilles, a warrior. Around 650 Greek manuscripts of it exist today, the earliest fragments coming from the third century BCE but most far later. The closest we have to a complete manuscript is from the ninth century CE. The events described in the *Iliad* took place during the Bronze Age and are commonly assumed to be c.1260–1180 BCE, with Homer writing about them much later; modelling based on the evolution of language suggests a date between 760 and 710 BCE. Note the wide gap between the events described and their writing (about five hundred years) and also the very long gap between the writing of the *Iliad* and our earliest existing manuscripts of it. And this, bar the Bible, is the best documentary evidence we have of any event from the ancient world.

By contrast, noted Princeton New Testament scholar Bruce Metzger comments that there are more than five thousand New Testament Greek catalogued manuscripts in existence today. Let the figure sink in: five thousand compared to the closet rival (the *Iliad*) at 650. This leads to Metzger's justified conclusion that 'The quantity of New Testament material is almost embarrassing in comparison with other works of antiquity'.[10]

But it is more than this, for the number of manuscripts is only part of the equation. The dating of them is equally (if not more) important. The closer the manuscript to the event described the better, for there is then less opportunity for errors in transmission or of a distortion of the facts.

The very oldest fragment of the Bible in existence today contains five verses from John's gospel, chapter 18. One of ninety-nine fragments from the New Testament that were written on papyrus and survive to this day, it is dated between 100 and 150 CE – in other words, within a hundred years of the events described, and the original from which it was copied would have been even closer to the events.

The bottom line is simply this. When it comes to material from the ancient world, nothing comes close to the Bible in terms of the number of manuscripts available or of their proximity to the actions described. While some might wish that we had the original gospels at our disposal, it doesn't get better than this when it comes to material from this period. If you are going to believe anything you read from the ancient world, you are on sound ground to privilege the manuscripts we have of the New Testament well ahead of any other. There simply are far, far more copies available, and those available are significantly closer to the events described. Another noted New Testament scholar, F.F. Bruce, sums up the evidence: 'There is no body of ancient literature in the world which enjoys such a wealth of good textual attestation as the New Testament.'[11]

While not in itself conclusive, the preservation of so many sections of the earliest biblical manuscripts could be seen to point to a hidden hand behind the process – not a conspiratorial hand (as per Dan Brown) but perhaps the very hand of God.

The Bible tells of many miracles; is it reasonable to believe that miracles happen?

Some object that while the Bible closely reflects the material written by the original authors, this does not make it credible. It simply means we have an accurate record of the original myths and fables they wrote. Put bluntly, just because we have the original record of a fable, it does not transform the fable into fact. An imaginative tale remains the product of a fertile imagination regardless of its dating or of how many times it is recorded.

Underlying this objection is the valid observation that much of the material recorded in the Bible tells of events so extraordinary that they have to be classified as miracles. Among other things, we are told of blind people who received their sight, of a donkey that spoke, of Jesus walking on water, of dead people coming back to life, and of the crucified Jesus conquering death and appearing to his disciples before ascending to heaven.

While there are those who accept that we have an essentially accurate record of the teaching of Jesus recorded in biblical passages such as the Sermon on the Mount, they find it impossible to accept the miracles recorded in the Bible, and are unwilling to accord Jesus any status above that of a specially talented Jewish rabbi who was willing to challenge the status quo and was ultimately crucified for his lack of diplomacy and tact.

Before we agree to this reduced understanding of Jesus, we need to contemplate how serious a shift this stance represents. After all, the gospels primarily record Jesus doing two things: teaching and going about performing miracles. If you rule the miracles out as impossible, what remains is effectively half of the material recorded about Jesus. That's a dramatically diminished account of his life – so diminished that you would question whether his message should be treated with anywhere near the seriousness that history has accorded to it. Furthermore, in the gospels his miracles help to give credence to his teaching. People in the narratives often wonder if the new ideas he puts forward have any validity, but in the face of the miraculous deeds they see, they conclude that they do. The pattern is fairly straightforward. You see it when he declares the sins of a paralysed man to be forgiven, and then validates the claim by healing the man from his paralysis (Mark 2:1–12). You spot it again in Mark 3:1–6 where Jesus challenges the Pharisees' understanding of the Jewish Sabbath laws and then heals a man's shrivelled hand on the Sabbath to add substance to his claim. Sometimes the link is even more dramatic, as in John 9:1–6 where the healing of the man born blind from birth vindicates Jesus' immediately prior claim to be 'the light of the world'.

Given this, I would argue that you cannot understand Jesus apart from his miracles. It is therefore important to investigate whether the thirty-seven miracles recorded in the gospels of Matthew, Mark, Luke and John are credible or not. If we conclude that they might well have happened, it seems reasonable to assume that the miracles recorded in other parts of the Bible might also be true.

It helps to start at the beginning and to ask why we find the idea of miracles to be problematic.

First we must briefly explain what we mean by 'miracles'. We should not confuse miracles with statistically rare events. For example, if the survival rate from a particularly vigorous form of cancer is one in a thousand, we should not proclaim a miracle if we know someone who survived that form of cancer. To the contrary, we should expect it to happen in one in a thousand cases, unless our original calculation of mathematical probability was inaccurate. Miracles are therefore not just rare events; they are events for which we can find no explanation other than by an appeal to something outside our current system of knowledge and understanding.

Though we may not know the term, most of us start with an uncritical embrace of the assumptions of **naturalism**, which is the belief that nature is a closed system with everything being explained by natural cause and effect. By definition, a miracle does not fit the usual rhythm of cause and effect, and therefore poses a challenge to this understanding of the world.

Not everyone accepts the assumptions of naturalism. It faces the difficulty of proclaiming that in a closed system nothing inherently new can happen, yet this flies in the face of the existence of the closed system itself. If nothing new can emerge, where did the system come from? How did it come into being? At some point it must have been new – the very thing that is supposed not to be possible.

Supernaturalism, by contrast, views nature as a sometimes open system, which, while usually operating by natural laws, is open to intervention by God. If you believe in the existence of God, particularly a God who created the 'closed box' of nature, it is possible that as creator, this God could intervene to modify laws of nature which usually serve the purposes of this God but from time to time might prove problematic and therefore be in need of temporary modification. If we live in a world where claims of the miraculous are made, and if these claims seem credible, it could well be that this is what is happening.

A common objection to miracles should be noted. Originally made by the Scottish philosopher David Hume, this argument maintains that it is always more likely that any claim to a miracle is false than that the miracle actually took place. As evidence, Hume cites the firm and unalterable laws of nature as testifying against any who claim a miraculous event. For example, if someone claims that a dead person has come back to life, the bodies of the billions of dead people who have never come back to life witness against the probability of the claim. The odds against the miracle being true are thus billions to one (billions of corpses versus one claim of a resurrection). However, this simply assumes that because something very rarely (if ever) happens, it cannot ever happen. But the argument is circular because by definition a miracle is something that goes against the flow of what we would usually expect to happen, and if we say that cannot happen, each time someone claims it *has* happened we declare them deluded or a liar. We do not actually weigh the evidence. We begin with the assumption that it must be false and allow nothing to count against that assumption. That is to be as closed in mindset as naturalism assumes the world of nature to be.

It is time to move this discussion of miracles in general to the miracles of Jesus. Besides the claim to be miraculous, some additional features are worth noting.

Jesus' miracles were usually performed in public. These were not mysterious deeds announced from behind closed doors. They were seen by many – at times by thousands. If they were fraudulent claims, there were more than enough people who could have come forward and denounced them with an 'I was there and that really did not happen'. Remember that the original records of the life of Jesus circulated during the lifetime of many who were present at the relevant events, so false or exaggerated claims could have been easily rebutted by the many witnesses. Simply put, these objections were not made.

At this point some might object and say, 'Yes, but you are talking about a primitive group of people whose understanding of the world was deeply superstitious and who could easily be deluded. No one claims that these people were intentionally deceitful or evil; they were simply ignorant and easy to fool.'

Perhaps, but don't be too quick to conclude that this argument is persuasive. The ancients were not as easily duped as we might think. Matthew 1:18–24 informs us that Joseph planned to break off his engagement to Mary when he heard of her pregnancy. Her claims of virginity did not impress him, as he was fully aware that virgins do not usually (ever) give birth. But something happened to change Joseph's mind. You might object that the something was a mere dream – and it was. But something about it was so compelling that he changed his position. If a witness is initially dubious as to the validity of a miraculous event but is forced by experience to change their perspective, it does strengthen the claim – though it might mean that it was a more sophisticated hoax than it originally appeared to be.

Was Joseph naive and deluded?

The rest of the story suggests he was anything but. Put differently, his default mindset in that unusual circumstance was exactly the same as ours would be in the twenty-first century. He was extremely sceptical. But something happened to change his natural scepticism to belief.

The fact that the person born from this alleged virgin birth went on to literally change the course of all human history could well be seen as a vindication of Joseph's change of perspective. After all, it is not every second Tuesday that someone like that is born. You have to be willing to ask whether something out of the ordinary might have been happening. Unless you assume that this is inherently impossible . . . But the world really did change as a result of the birth of Jesus and there is no getting away from that.

Much depends on your starting point.

If you start with the assumption that Jesus could not possibly have been the Son of God and that miracles do not happen, you have no choice but to discard the miracles of Jesus as fables. You do so not because you have carefully considered the evidence for the claims but because you have started with an unshakable conviction: miracles do not happen, therefore any claim of a miracle must be false.

If by contrast you are willing to entertain the possibility that Jesus is the Son of God, the miracles assume a very different role. If God was indeed intervening in the world in a decisive way, it is not at all surprising to suggest that this would be heralded by signs (miracles) that would attract our attention. While the gospels portray Jesus as being a persuasive and brilliant teacher, they are insistent that he was more than this. His teaching was backed up by signs that attested to his authority. Nature listened when he spoke (as, for example, when he calmed a storm at sea), the sick were healed, demons were silenced, dead people were restored to life, and a new order of reality was ushered in by Jesus' miraculous resurrection from the dead.

You can't separate the identity of Jesus from his miracles. The gospels provide four eyewitness accounts of the life and ministry of Jesus. They don't all recount exactly the same miracles; sometimes a miracle is described by only one gospel writer, sometimes two or three, and in the case of the feeding of the five thousand and the resurrection, by all four. But the bottom line is essentially the same. Each account portrays Jesus as someone who went about both teaching and performing miracles. And each is equally adamant that as a result of his ministry he was crucified, but then had his ministry dramatically vindicated by God through his resurrection from the dead.

It is to this miracle – the miracle of all miracles – that we now turn. As we look at it, the stakes are high. The apostle Paul was adamant when he wrote in 1 Corinthians 15:17, 'If Christ has not been raised, your faith is futile' and then in verse 19 expanded further: 'If only for this life we have hope in Christ, we are to be pitied more than all others' (TNIV). Paul knew what he was talking about. He, like many of the early Christians, had staked his life on the resurrection of Jesus. He was to die as a result of proclaiming it. And he fully understood that if his belief in the resurrection was misguided, he would have sacrificed his life for a hoax. If it was a hoax, as he said, 'we are to be pitied more than all others'.

Not that he believed for one moment that it was a delusion. He went on to announce his strong conviction: 'But Christ has indeed been raised from the dead, the firstfruits of those who have fallen asleep' (1 Corinthians 15:20).

Let's explore why Paul was so sure that this miracle had taken place.

What are we to make of the claim that Jesus was resurrected from the dead?

Graffiti was an art form during my university days. It adorned three of the walls of every toilet cubicle. One wall was devoted to political comment, another to the smutty, the third to the witty and clever. By and large contributors conformed to this unwritten guideline, and a few days before a now long past Easter a headline appeared on the third wall: 'Easter has been cancelled. They've found the body!' It has stuck with me through the years.

In its own way, the witty comment is deeply insightful. Produce the body of Jesus, and while the impact of Christianity would not disappear overnight, its reason for being would. True, Christianity has been a force for moral good in the world, and so some might feel that though it was built on a lie (the resurrection of Jesus), the end justifies the means. But most would not assess it like this. We have already noted the apostle Paul's assessment in 1 Corinthians 15:17,19: 'If Christ has not been raised, your faith is futile . . . If only for this life we have hope in Christ, we are to be pitied more than all others.'

Why pitied? Well, it's pretty pathetic to build your life on an illusion, and if Christ is not the death-transcending victor proclaimed in Christianity, then there truly has been much ado about nothing.

So what are we to make of the claim that Jesus was resurrected from the dead?

First of all let's note what *isn't* being claimed. Jesus didn't come back from the dead. The Bible gives accounts of others who did, Jesus himself restoring Jairus's daughter to life (Mark 5:21–43) and calling

Lazarus back from the grave (John 11:1–44). Both went on to die again at a time and date now unknown to us.

By contrast, Jesus returns to his disciples in his resurrection body, effectively showing us what we can expect our bodies to be like on the other side of death. Again it is Paul who is so perceptive about this when he writes 'Christ has indeed been raised from the dead, the firstfruits of those who have fallen asleep' (1 Corinthians 15:20). In other words, Christ is the first in the harvest that still awaits. Just as he has been raised from the dead, so shall all those who place their trust and faith in Jesus. Like Jesus, they will have a body that is both similar and dissimilar to their present body. The disciples were able to recognize the resurrected Jesus, but it took a while. And the biblical accounts record that the resurrected Jesus could enter a room through locked doors and appear and disappear rapidly. Similarity and difference. Not back from the dead to live on this planet for a little longer, but appearing from the other side of death giving a foretaste of what awaits. It is the triumphant announcement not of the end of death but that death is not the end.

While this might sound inspiring, there is a pressing question to ask: is there any evidence for the resurrection of Jesus?

First, the obvious answer. Easter has never been cancelled because the body has never been produced.

True, there could be a range of reasons for this. We have all heard of cases where someone is assumed dead but a lingering doubt remains because no corpse has been located. While not common, it happens from time to time.

Not that we should be too quick to assume that the disappearance of Jesus' body is insignificant. Something must have happened to it. What? Why couldn't they find it? And let's be clear about this: as the fledgling Christian faith grew, there was plenty of motivation to find it. If the leaders of his time found Jesus so troublesome that they crucified him, it turned out he was even more troublesome after his death. His teaching simply wouldn't disappear and was elevated to the indisputable by the claim that the grave had proved incapable of holding him captive. It would have been so helpful to the enemies of the early church to have been able to produce his body before the story caught hold. But they didn't, presumably because they couldn't. Interesting.

Second, there is the clear change in the lives of his disciples. By all accounts they were at best a pretty ordinary bunch. Indeed, the case can be made that they were somewhat below average. After all, while most of them were fishermen, the Bible never records an account of them catching any fish without Jesus first performing a miracle. Average fishermen catch fish on their own. They were probably wise to have changed careers. I guess this is why Paul is a little disparaging in his description of the early church: 'Not many of you were wise by human standards; not many were influential; not many were of noble birth. But God chose the foolish things of the world to shame the wise; God chose the weak things of the world to shame the strong' (1 Corinthians 1:26–27). But the bottom line, and an indisputable truth, is that this somewhat below average group of people went on to decisively change all of human history, and that for the good.

How did they do it? Realistically, if you were a gambler you wouldn't have backed them. The smart money was on Christianity never surviving long enough to become Christianity. Everyone assumed that post crucifixion, this brilliant but disturbing teacher from Nazareth would be quietly forgotten, his former followers again pursuing unsuccessful careers in fishing.

Something happened to change them. They were very clear as to what it was. They claimed that they had met the resurrected Jesus. Even the most sceptical of them, Thomas, recounted how he had been invited to touch the pierced hands and side of Jesus. At that point he stopped doubting (John 20:24–29). The transformation that came over the disciples was staggering. Filled with courage, they boldly proclaimed the resurrection of Jesus. They did it with a conviction that others found compelling. And they did it at the cost of their own lives. Of the original eleven apostles who witnessed the resurrected Jesus, all but John were to be executed for insisting on telling this story, and John was to be imprisoned on the island of Patmos for his emphatic refusal to renounce his conviction that he had seen the risen Jesus.

Was it sheer stubbornness on their part? All earlier portraits of the disciples show them to be fickle people, so realistically, that is unlikely.

Were they inherently suicidal, intent on martyrdom? There is always the possibility that one or two might have been, but to claim that all of them were is a bit of a stretch, don't you think?

Were they gullible and deluded, fooled by who knows what trickery? Perhaps. Clearly something happened, so it would be interesting to know what it was. If trickery, it wasn't a one-off conjuring act. There were several resurrection appearances, and each was found to be convincing. So who did it? Clearly not Jesus if he was dead. So who? And why? Let's face it, to assume some deliberate hoax takes a fair stretch of imagination.

Something happened post crucifixion. We know it did, because there is no disputing the transformation that took place in the disciples. Whatever it was, it was so powerful that it led to the transformation of the world. That is something out of the ordinary.

The explanation of the first disciples has become the explanation given by the church through the centuries: Christ has died, Christ is risen, Christ will come again. That account continues to resonate deep in the human heart. It could well be that it does so because it is true.

Oh, and by the way, Easter remains a firm calendar booking. There is still no body to show.

What are we to make of the church?

Living as we do in the twenty-first century, we have become used to the existence of the church. It simply is, and has been for the last two thousand years. We know that the Christian faith is both the largest and the most widespread of the world's religions, with approximately one third of the world's population claiming some form of allegiance to it, although for many that allegiance is fairly nominal (the attitude often being, 'Given that I'm not Hindu, Jewish or Muslim, presumably I'm Christian'). We probably don't probe deeply into how the church came into existence, and if we did, we would do so with the assumption that a series of highly favourable circumstances combined together to ensure the birth of this most successful of all religions. And our assumption would be entirely wrong.

Though Judaism at its birth was mandated with the task of being a global religion, its founder Abram being told at his call that 'all peoples on earth will be blessed through you' (Genesis 12:3), in practice it was an essentially insular faith. While it allowed those who were not Jewish by birth to convert to Judaism, the obstacles to entry were high (including circumcision for male converts), and no serious effort was made to convert the nations surrounding Israel to Judaism. At its foundation, Christianity was essentially a small and insignificant sect of Judaism. Its founder Jesus taught a different understanding of the Jewish faith from that customarily taught in the Jewish synagogues, and a series of all too many conflicts with the Jewish authorities had seen them organize his crucifixion.

Jesus' execution should have been the last word on his life. This was an unsettled period of Jewish history, much of the unsettlement being related to the Roman conquest and occupation of Israel. So horrific and distasteful was the Roman control of Israel that many Jews believed the time was ripe for God to send the promised Messiah – someone who would release Israel from the bondage in which it found itself. There were several messianic-style preachers at the time of Jesus. It was not unusual for them to gather a crowd of supporters around them, but the outcome was always one of two: initial bursts of enthusiasm either died out as a result of waning interest, or they were systematically crushed. The crucifixion of Jesus indicates that the unsettlement that resulted from his itinerant preaching was of a sufficient order to require stronger measures, and the expectation would have been that Jesus would simply fall into the category of a Jewish protester who had been silenced by force – one of several who needed to be dealt with in this manner to enable the status quo to continue unhindered.

If anyone had been told that Jesus' teaching would continue after his crucifixion, they would have been surprised, no doubt assuming it would be a local affair limited to the nation of Israel. They would surmise that against the odds he had succeeded in creating a new branch of thought within Judaism, perhaps a sect of Judaism. No one would have expected the founding of a world religion, one that two thousand years after the birth of Jesus is larger and more widely spread than it has ever been before. Given that the focus of Judaism had been parochial and exclusive throughout its history, and that all the original followers of Christianity were Jewish (as was Jesus), there was nothing to suggest that this faith would go global and transform the world.

What happened?

If we are to believe the accounts of the life of Jesus found in the gospels of Matthew, Mark, Luke and John (and we will find no more reliable guide from this period of history), Jesus deliberately focused his ministry and attention on his Jewish audience. Though he did not exclude interested foreigners, he did not encourage their involvement and appeared to tolerate it rather than welcome it.

There are a few examples that can be pointed to, but Matthew 15:21–28 is as good as any. The passage claims that a Canaanite woman came to Jesus and begged him to heal her demon-possessed daughter. Jesus' initial response to her was 'I was sent only to the lost sheep of Israel' (v. 24); in other words, 'As a Canaanite you fall outside my mandated mission, and I am therefore not authorized to help you.' The woman is not easily dissuaded (which, given her desperation, is understandable), and makes a simple raw appeal 'Lord, help me!' (v. 25). Jesus then gives a provocative reply; indeed, it seems harsh and lacking in empathy: 'It is not right to take the children's bread and toss it to the dogs' (v. 26). Put differently, 'I'm here for the Jews. You Canaanite dogs can find your own Messiah.' Swallowing any national pride she might have had, the woman counters, 'Even the dogs eat the crumbs that fall from their master's table' (v. 27). The answer impresses Jesus, especially as it indicates the great faith she places in his ability to cure her child, and he announces that the woman's daughter is healed. The passage goes on to affirm that the girl's healing took place the instant that Jesus proclaimed it.

Whatever we might make of this passage, it is clear that at this stage Jesus considered that the focus of his ministry needed to be on the Jewish community. His response was typically Jewish for that time. Jews did not forbid Gentiles from converting to Judaism, but they certainly didn't make it easy for them. If you were a Gentile you had to be persistent (and probably a little desperate) to overcome the barriers to entry. It is not just in the twenty-first century that people are suspicious of foreigners.

What caused the shift in focus?

Again, if we are to believe the account of the mission of Jesus found in the gospels, and if we supplement this record with the history of the early church as recorded in the Acts of the Apostles, we find a marked shift in strategy after the crucifixion and alleged resurrection of Jesus.

Matthew 28:19 records the resurrected Jesus instructing his disciples to 'go and make disciples of all nations', while in the Acts of the Apostles Luke informs us that Jesus' closing words to his disciples prior to his ascension into heaven were 'You will be my witnesses in Jerusalem, and in all Judea and Samaria, and to the ends of the earth' (Acts 1:8).

It would appear then that Jesus saw his initial mission as an outreach to the people of Israel, but that after the resurrection this broadens to include 'the ends of the earth'.

We should not underestimate how significant this shift in focus was, and how difficult it was to achieve.

Much of the history of the early church as recorded in the New Testament is a record of it adjusting to this new focus. The fledgling church birthed after the death of Jesus was initially a branch of Judaism. Almost all its followers were Jewish, and its first regular place of meeting was in the Jewish temple courts (Acts 2:46). There was a deep reluctance to incorporate Gentiles into the life of the church, and Acts 10 records a special vision received by the first leader of the church, the apostle Peter, validating outreach to non-Jews. The initial vision was further vindicated when Gentile converts received the Holy Spirit, Acts 10:45 recording the surprise among the early believers 'that the gift of the Holy Spirit had been poured out even on Gentiles'. These were paradigm-changing events. They underlined that the message of Jesus was not just for Jews but for the whole world.

This new emphasis was significantly accelerated as a result of the missionary work of the apostle Paul among the Gentiles. The role of Paul in spreading Christianity beyond the parameters of Judaism cannot be overestimated. As a champion of the Gentiles, Paul managed to get the early church to reconsider its position on the reception of these new converts into the previously almost exclusively Jewish Christian church. As a result of his work (and some bitter battles), it was agreed that male Gentile converts did not need to be circumcised. The guiding principle is summed up in Acts 15:19: 'we should not make it difficult for the Gentiles who are turning to God.' Once that principle was adopted, Christianity started to spread fairly rapidly among non-Jewish communities. It was only a matter of time until the number of Christians from a Gentile background outnumbered the number of Christians from a Jewish background.

It also marked a shift in the thinking of the early Christians. Like most of the Jews at the time, they linked the coming of a Jewish Messiah to the overthrow of the Romans, and to the return of a period akin to when King David had been their leader. This golden era for Israel was looked back on with great nostalgia and longing. If God had simply let them return to the freedom and influence the nation had enjoyed at that time, most would have died happy.

Initially the early Christians had assumed this is what was going to take place with the resurrection of Jesus. The disciples' last recorded conversation with Jesus prior to his ascension is found in Acts 1:6 when they pointedly ask him, 'Lord, are you at this time going to restore the kingdom to Israel?' This was the focus of their concern and they wanted to know when their country would be free again. Jesus sidesteps the question and says instead, 'You will be my witnesses in

Jerusalem, and in all Judea and Samaria, and to the ends of the earth'
(Acts 1:8).

Now it is true that it took a while for the significance of Jesus' last
words to sink in, and it was only with the advent of the missionary
work of Paul that this vision started to materialize. But consider how
large a shift in thinking it required. Once Gentiles entered the church
in large numbers the agenda of the church ceased to be about the fortunes of Israel, and the focus became the concerns of the wider world.
Indeed, as large numbers of Romans converted to Christianity, the
attention could no longer be on defeating the Romans but on living
in the light of the teaching of Jesus. Put differently, the emphasis
became the kingdom of God rather than the well-being of Israel.

Pause for a moment. If this shift had not taken place, Christianity
almost certainly would have faded out of existence as a colourful
but irrelevant sect of Judaism. All of human history was significantly impacted by Paul's decision to primarily focus his missionary
endeavours among the Gentiles. It could so easily not have happened.
Was that a result of God's intervention, or did Christianity strike it
lucky? Let's be clear: at the time no one would have realized the full
impact of the shift or had any idea how dramatically it would change
the course of history. This was not a carefully thought through and
implemented strategy. It was a fresh new direction followed as a result
of the visionary last statement of Jesus and the deep convictions of
the apostle Paul.

The Bible's own account of the ministry of Paul is that it was
miraculously initiated by God. If we are to believe the Bible's portrait of what occurred, prior to his conversion Paul was fanatically
committed to the Jewish cause, so much so that he participated in
the arrest and persecution of Jews who had converted to Christianity.
Acts 7:54 – 8:3 informs us that Saul ('Saul' is the Jewish version of his
name and 'Paul' the Latin version which was used in his work among
the Gentiles) was present at the stoning of the first Christian mar-
tyr Stephen, and that after Stephen's death he intensified his efforts
against the early church, or to quote Acts 8:3 'began to destroy the
church'.

That changed as a result of events recorded in Acts 9, when on a journey to arrest Christians who had fled to Damascus he had a vision from heaven. A sudden flash of light was accompanied by a voice from heaven asking 'Saul, Saul, why do you persecute me?' When Saul asks who the 'me' refers to, the voice replies that it is Jesus. Everything changes for Saul as a result of this dramatic encounter. He shifts from being the persecutor of the church to a champion of its cause, and later to the champion of its cause among the Gentiles.

We can of course dismiss the Bible's account of what happened as a fanciful fabrication to give some legitimacy to Paul's ministry, and especially to his claim to be considered an apostle. While the other apostles were able to validate their ministry by pointing to their association with Jesus during his life, Paul was able to point to this special encounter with Christ as being the equivalent.

Such scepticism is probably unwarranted. The proof of the validity of Paul's call is seen in the impact of his ministry. He wrote a large section of the New Testament, and no one saw more churches planted than he did, and that in many diverse locations. Take Paul out of the equation and it is highly improbable that Christianity would exist today. If you are asking simply whether Christianity is probably true, assess whether the ministry of Paul is best categorized as a lucky break for the church, or whether it could possibly be the result of the hand of God at work. Luck or God?

While I have emphasized the importance of Paul to the long-term survival of Christianity, the story is yet more enthralling. While the apostle Paul broadened the base and appeal of the church, its continued survival amid vigorous opposition and persecution by a series of Roman emperors, from Nero onwards, also needs to be noted and thought through.

The first wave of persecution faced by the early church was initiated by its Jewish detractors. An incited Jewish mob was responsible for the arrest and prosecution of Stephen before the members of the Jewish Sanhedrin (Acts 6:8–15), while King Herod had James the brother of John beheaded and, noting that this met with the approval of the Jews, continued his assault on the church (Acts 12:1–4). In the early stages opposition to Christianity was thus primarily linked to the opposition of the Jews, who wanted to ensure that Christianity did not become a new Jewish sect.

This changed on 19 July 64, when a great fire destroyed much of Rome. The Roman emperor Nero was rumoured to have started the fire – in order to clear sections of the city so that he could then erect impressive new buildings in his honour – but things had got out of hand. Certainly the fire was devastating in its effect, with ten of the fourteen quarters within Rome affected. It was necessary to find someone to blame. In the past, Jewish militants had used arson to retaliate against Rome, and initially Nero focused his gaze on them, but they managed to deflect his attention to the emerging Christian faith, which was significantly more vulnerable and exposed. Thus began the first major wave of persecution faced on a large scale by Christians. Many were tortured and put to death in the Roman arena.

In one form or another, the persecution of the church continued for well over 250 years. Its intensity varied during this time, and for some periods it was relatively mild. Likewise, attacks were sometimes localized, with the new faith actively opposed in some parts of the empire but treated more sedately in others. The unevenness of the persecution helped the church to consolidate and pick itself up again after periods of ferocious attack. The remarkable thing is that the church not only survived but saw consistent growth. It was so surprising that Tertullian (c.155–c.240), often called the father of Latin Christianity, in his *Apologeticus* wrote the oft-cited words, 'The blood of the martyrs is the seed of the church.' Tertullian's work was a vigorous defence of Christianity and a plea that it be granted the same legal status as other sects which were tolerated by the Roman Empire. His cry in the closing chapter gives a sense of the urgency of the time: 'Crucify us – torture us – condemn us – destroy us! Your injustice is the proof of our innocence . . . When we are condemned by you, we are acquitted by God.'[12] It is rousing stuff, but led to no immediate termination of persecution.

Pause again for a while and consider the enormity of the challenge faced by the early church. By and large its members were ordinary people of little or no social standing in the broader society. Many were slaves. It was persecuted for a sustained period – not one generation but almost nine (about 260 years). You would not have expected it to survive, but it did.

Why?

Various answers are given.

Some note the quality of life among the early Christians. They genuinely cared for their widows and orphans, and for the sick and frail in their midst. They shared that care with those outside their immediate circle. We may think there is nothing remarkable about this, but that is because we live in a world that has been shaped by the presuppositions of Christianity, where love for one's neighbour is commanded and even taken for granted. No such world existed before the advent of Christianity. Genuine care, especially for those outside your kinship, was virtually unheard of. It proved to be attractive, and impacted the ancient world, leading to the growth of Christianity.

The early church also took a stance against adultery, abortion and infanticide. It was not uncommon for Christians to rescue babies that had been abandoned at birth and to raise them as their own. A watching world was bemused, perhaps even confused, but over time was convinced that this was a religion of love. They had seen nothing like it before. Rodney Stark, a sociologist of religion, has calculated that the sheer winsomeness of Christianity saw it grow rapidly in spite of persecution. He suggests a figure of about 40% growth per decade for the first few hundred years.[13]

If the quality of the lives of the early Christians was a major factor in the growth of the church, there were other more down-to-earth considerations.

Though the Roman Empire could be harsh and brutal towards its opponents, it was essentially so strong at the time of the birth of the church that the then known world experienced a long period of peace, the Pax Romana (or the Pax Augusta as it is also known), which lasted from around 27 BCE to 180 CE. During this period the Roman Empire had a population of about 70 million, most of whom enjoyed these years of peace. An excellent system of Roman roads made travel around the empire relatively easy. Add to this the wide-spread acceptance of Latin as a language, and the setting was ripe for the movement of people and thus the spread of ideas which at another time would have remained localized and been hard to disseminate. In other words, if you wanted to birth a global religion, this was a good time to do it. People could move around relatively safely, share ideas, and be understood by a wide number of people as a result of an almost universal language. Such fortuitous circumstances had never existed before.

That there was a religion (Christianity) waiting to spread rapidly can be seen as a happy coincidence, or we could attach a faith factor to it and suggest that in this we see the hand of God. The decision boils down to lucky timing, or the hand of God. We can't be dogmatic about either, but we should note that when we rule out the God hypothesis, we often have to appeal to luck. At what point does this appeal start to wear thin?

The persecution of the Christian church ceased after the conversion of the Roman emperor Constantine the Great in 312. In 313 Constantine issued the Edict of Milan, granting toleration to Christians and members of other religions. He also forbade Jews from stoning to death other Jews who converted to Christianity. Constantine's programme was one of religious freedom, and he supported both Christianity and paganism.

Under the emperor's protection, Christian leaders for the first time could gather to consider their faith and its major teachings. A council was convened by Constantine from 20 May to 19 June 325 in the Bithynian city of Nicaea. Thought to have been attended by 318 church leaders, the Council of Nicea provided an opportunity for the bishops to discuss their common understanding of Christian doctrine and led to clarification on the divine nature of Jesus and his relationship to God the Father. It also produced the Nicene Creed, the first creedal statement to define the key beliefs of Christianity. It is hard to overestimate how significant this event was in producing a common understanding of the Christian faith. The previous history of persecution had made any such gathering impossible, indeed even inconceivable. This was a major breakthrough.

An even more remarkable history lay ahead. Though Constantine is often credited with making Christianity the official religion of the Roman Empire, this is not true. His prime contribution was to insist on religious toleration. In fact, there is some debate as to how genuine Constantine's conversion to Christianity was. He seems to have hedged his bets, and in 314 added depictions of the cross to his coins but also the pagan figures of Sol Invictus and Mars Conservator. Clearly his was not an exclusive allegiance to Christianity.

The shift from toleration of Christianity to adopting it as the official religion of Rome was made by Emperor Theodosius, who in 380 issued the Edict of Thessalonica, making Christianity the sole authorized religion of the empire. Whereas Christianity was no longer illegal after the conversion of Constantine, this was a far more significant step. Post Theodosius, you had to be a Christian if you wanted any future in Rome. It appears that Theodosius took this step because he was a genuine believer and wanted all his subjects to have a complete trust in Jesus. Which makes what happens next so intriguing.

This is how I tell it in my book, *The Big Picture*:[14]

In 390 a charioteer in Thessalonica was accused of homosexual behaviour. The governor of the district had him imprisoned, but the people of the area, who enjoyed his charioteering skills, demanded his release. The governor refused, leading to an uprising in which the governor was killed and the arrested man set free. Incensed on hearing this, Emperor Theodosius, who had been instrumental in having Christianity decreed as the official religion of the Roman Empire, ordered that the residents of the area be punished. At a chariot race in Thessalonica, Theodosius's soldiers trapped those attending inside, and within three hours had slaughtered around seven thousand people.

Ambrose, the Bishop of Milan, was appalled at this indiscriminate slaughter, and in the name of the church called on Theodosius to repent. Initially Theodosius refused, and consequently Ambrose would not give him communion. Theodosius stayed away from church for a while, but his commitment to the faith made this situation untenable. He reluctantly accepted Ambrose's terms for reconciliation, which included the promotion of a law which required a delay of thirty days before any death sentence passed would be enforced. In front of a crowded congregation, Theodosius took off his imperial robes and asked for forgiveness of his sins. Ambrose initially declined to offer this, but after Theodosius had repeatedly requested it, at a church service on Christmas day Ambrose gave Theodosius the sacrament.

Shelley comments on the significance of this, 'It required unusual courage to humiliate a Byzantine emperor. Ambrose had hit upon the weapon – the threat of excommunication – which the Western church would soon use again and again to humble princes.'[15] The emperor could frighten people into obedience with the sword, but the church could determine their eternal destiny. This made the church more powerful than the emperor.

Most commentators then focus on later church–state struggles and the growing power that the church gained. And fair enough; this is a good incident to point back to. After all, you can hardly have imagined a Nero or a Diocletian crawling on hands and knees to beg forgiveness of a bishop of the church. Roman emperors saw no need to answer to anyone. They were considered gods, so why would they?

However, instead of running decades ahead and speculating about the later implications of this encounter, we should evaluate it against its own time.

Reflect upon the courage it took for Ambrose to confront a Roman emperor and to excommunicate him, especially as this was the emperor who had declared Christianity the official religion of his empire. Theodosius might have been sympathetic to the work of the church, but it was improbable that he would be so sympathetic that he would accept such a rebuke meekly. Ambrose's action was undoubtedly brave – but was it not also reckless, perhaps even irresponsible? He could have catapulted the church back into an era of persecution and oppression. You simply did not confront a Roman emperor and live. No exceptions.

So why did Ambrose excommunicate this essentially pious emperor?

Ambrose himself wrote of the event: 'When a priest does not talk to a sinner, then the sinner will die in his sin, and the priest will be guilty because he failed to correct him.'[16] In short, 'I am a priest; the emperor was a sinner; I spoke to him as someone who needed to find forgiveness.' The tone is pastoral, as is the motivation.

But why did Ambrose see this as such a great evil? This wasn't the twenty-first century. Life was cheap; tragedy was common. Why was Ambrose so outraged?

Because seven thousand people had been slaughtered. While Ambrose did not know each person who was killed, he knew that each was known to God. He knew that every individual is precious to God and made in God's image. And he knew that if this now supposedly Christian empire was to stand for anything, it needed a higher standard of justice and compassion than this. He knew that no one could be above the law, because no one is above God – not even the emperor. In short, his Christian convictions compelled him to act, regardless of the risk.

Today we are outraged when we hear of atrocities and injustice, and rightly so. But from where does that outrage flow? Ambrose versus Theodosius reminds us that when the Roman Empire embraced Christianity it embarked upon a journey that had never previously been trodden. It was a journey where every life mattered and where no one was above the law. Holding power was no longer seen as an excuse for abusing power. To the contrary, to hold power was to hold a sacred trust from God and therefore to be eternally accountable.

We should be thankful to Ambrose for his extraordinary courage in seeing questions of justice so clearly. And we should be equally grateful that Theodosius, even though the emperor, and one who had failed a moral test most dismally, had the integrity and courage to seek the forgiveness of God, for he believed that God knows and understands every human heart.

While it is true that Ambrose versus Theodosius established a precedent for later church–state conflicts where the church acted a lot less honourably, it is helpful to remember that this is how it started – with the church holding the moral high ground and courageously acting on behalf of those who were vulnerable and unable to defend themselves. This was the nature of the church community that had been birthed.

Sudden access to power and influence saw more than a few compromises over the following centuries, but the story of the first four hundred years or so is impressive. It is a story of great courage and of offering a genuinely alternative way of living, a completely different vision of the purpose and nature of life. It is a story of the slow capturing of the heart and imagination of society, and of doing so against the odds.

It is also a story that requires some explanation. Was it just a lucky break – a new moral force slowly filtering through society in reaction to an increasingly corrupt and decaying Roman Empire? Or should we read something more into it? Could it be that this was the fulfilment of Jesus' own prophecy, recorded in Acts 1:8, that his disciples would be witnesses to his message in Jerusalem, Judea, Samaria and to the ends of the earth? It is beyond dispute that this prophecy has come true, but is that just because of luck, or should we see the hand of God behind it?

It is time to assess where our arguments from chapters 2 and 3 leave us. But that requires a new chapter.

4

Let's Weigh This Up

I still remember my first science teacher at high school.

Mr Bell was an avowed atheist and had a flair for the sensational. One day he announced that he would prove to us the non-existence of God.

'If there is a God,' he declared, 'I'll give him or her a chance to prove their existence. Look under my desk. You can see there is no money there.'

And he gave us all an opportunity to check, and to declare that there was indeed no hidden cash supply lying under his table.

'Now,' declared Mr Bell, 'I'll give God an opportunity. I'll believe that God exists if within the next two minutes a supply of banknotes appears under my desk.'

He dramatically counted off the 120 seconds he had given for God to act, and then ducked under his desk, peering in every nook and cranny and loudly proclaiming, 'Well, there is no money there. Such a pity. Such a pity.'

As 12-year-olds, we found this most amusing, and a lot more entertaining than studying the periodic table, so we laughed along, ensuring the experiment lasted for most of the science period.

At the end Mr Bell announced, 'No money. No God. Case proved.'

I certainly don't want to suggest that most atheists would agree with Mr Bell's approach, and even as an adolescent I found his argument far from convincing. While loving the sense of drama Mr Bell added to each lesson, I doubted his logic. If a God did exist, why would that God feel obligated to produce a wad of banknotes just because my science teacher had asked for it? And if the banknotes *had* appeared, wouldn't that imply that Mr Bell was in charge of God, as he would have been the one to set the agenda for God rather than, as one would have expected, God being the one to decide what would or wouldn't happen. While providing some light entertainment, it was an irrelevant experiment. Though it taught me little about science, it did leave me thinking.

There was a basic point behind Mr Bell's antics. Why is the existence of God not a little more obvious? If there is a God who wants us to believe that he, she or it exists, why not be a bit more obliging and perhaps turn up for a conversation at reasonably regular intervals? That way, everyone would have no trouble in believing, and all doubt could be removed.

In principle, it was perhaps the same point made by the cosmonaut Yuri Gagarin in the first human journey into space, when he allegedly commented, 'I see no God up here.' While it later transpired that the claim came not from Gagarin but as a piece of propaganda from the then Soviet president, Nikita Khrushchev, let's not split hairs. After all, if Gagarin had said it, it would have been true. There was no God to be spotted when the previous confines of the earth were shattered and we entered space. And again, the little point begs to be made: if there is a God, why is it not more obvious?

As we have been examining evidence both for and against the existence of God, a quick summary of where we have arrived is in order.

For atheists, the issue is not so much that they find reasons not to believe in God, but rather that in the absence of what they would consider to be compelling evidence for God's existence (such as the arrival of a wad of banknotes in response to a wager), they find it unnecessary to pose the God hypothesis – in much the same way as I may say that as no one has ever given me any reason to believe that I have fairies dancing at the bottom of my garden, I see no reason to get into a discussion on the likelihood of them being there. Put differently, and to quote the slogan: 'Absence of evidence is evidence of absence.' Why suggest that someone or something exists when there is nothing to suggest that this is the case?

True, most atheists would acknowledge that the sheer fact of our existence does pose a problem. While non-existence would require no explanation, the reality of life on this planet (and especially conscious life) requires some commentary.

They would, however, suggest that while the God hypothesis was a suitable cop-out in an era where few facts were known and science was a mystery, we now live in an age where we are increasingly confident of having a reasonable explanation for the origin of life that is in no way dependent on the existence of any god or gods. They would go further and argue that if God actually does exist this would introduce an additional layer of complexity, for then we would have to find an explanation for God's life. Rather than providing a solution to the question of existence, the God hypothesis confuses the issue and creates more problems than it solves. Alternatively, we could say that the God hypothesis has little explanatory power and should therefore be rejected.

Those who believe in God's existence, and who in addition suggest that the Christian understanding of God and reality is probably essentially true, find this argument underwhelming. They dispute the foundational premise that there is no evidence which points to the existence of God. They would go so far as to argue that the evidence is everywhere to be spotted, and, to quote the saying, 'There are none so blind as those who will not see.'

What is it that they see as they look at the world with eyes that focus differently?

They see a world of order, beauty and complexity – a world that so nearly didn't come into existence. They read the scientific data which suggests that life would never have originated if the earth were tilted at a slightly different angle, or if it were a little further from or closer to the sun, or if there had been an additional moon, or some other 'if', and they note how incredibly long this list of happy coincidences is.

More fundamentally, they see the pre-existence of laws which underlie every explanation for the origin of the universe. At the very least they note that before anything was, some guiding laws were in place to determine the evolutionary pathway of whatever happened to exist, no matter how infinitesimally small it might have been. Are we to assume that these laws simply were? To postulate laws without a lawmaker is problematic, so there is nothing inherently illogical about exploring the possible existence of a lawmaker. This is not akin to trying to find fairies at the bottom of the garden. The world does exist, and any explanation that attempts to avoid answering how the laws of science came into being is a non-answer and sidesteps a most critical question.

Though this argument has been advanced with many additional twists and nuances, it is essentially the one put forward by Thomas Aquinas, who argued that existence presupposes a necessary first being who is uncreated and who is the creator of every other being. The evidence for this is life itself, and this is made even more compelling when we consider how intricate and complex life is. There is a necessary first cause behind everything, and this first cause is God.

This argument is further strengthened by the widespread acceptance of broad moral precepts. From whence has morality been derived, especially as it has no obvious evolutionary purpose (the survival of the fittest more naturally inclining us to expect a ruthless planet)? Are we to believe that in spite of the world appearing to be created (because it is well ordered and clearly fit for purpose), this is simply good fortune, and that a near universal morality is also a surprising but fortuitous chance? Those unable to see any design behind creation require us to believe that we have been incredibly lucky, and the odds against this being the case are mounting.

The case for theism takes an additional step forward when we explore the case for Christian theism.

We examined the witness of the Bible.

It is simply true to say that no other book has impacted life on this planet as much as this one. When atheists suggest that they would be willing to believe in God if only he or she was prepared to turn up for a regular chat, the Bible notes that in principle, God has already done so. It recounts one 'God turned up' account after another. The book is filled with God stories, and we must decide if we should dismiss them all, or if, at least in some instances, something noteworthy actually happened. At the very least we must acknowledge that when we compare belief in God to belief in fairies at the bottom of the garden, there is this distinctive difference: vast numbers of people have claimed a God encounter. The particular stories recorded in the Bible have been retained because those who were alive at the time found these accounts to be particularly compelling. Rather than looking at an absence of evidence, we are perhaps looking at an embarrassment of evidence – so much of it, from so many different sources, over so many different centuries.

To dismiss the evidence with a 'But that's the Bible. Who would believe that?' misses the point. These stories have taken on a power and life of their own. They have shaped the world as we know it. Why? There are many fine works of literature. They have had nowhere near the same influence. Christians maintain that God has been behind the incredible success of the Bible. While they believe that ordinary people wrote its various books, they are convinced that quietly behind the scenes God was at work, using the personalities of the different authors to produce a richly textured and fully inspired book, the inspiration coming from none other than God. They find any other explanation for the lasting impact of the Bible to be deficient.

It's another point to ponder.

Some object that the Bible recounts many miracles and therefore could not possibly be true. The argument they put forward goes something like this.

'Well, that clearly didn't happen.'

'Why not?'

'Because if it did, it would be a miracle.'

'What's the problem with that?'

'Miracles don't happen.'

'But this one just did. Didn't you hear the account?'

'It couldn't possibly be true, because miracles do not happen.'

Notice that none of this is about evidence. It is about firmly held beliefs that are not willing to weigh evidence. No one suggests that miracles come as anything but a surprise. Our natural default reaction is towards scepticism or to find another explanation. But there are times when no satisfactory alternative explanation can be found. We then have to query the validity of our first assumption that miracles do not happen.

This is most clearly demonstrated in the miracle of the resurrection of Jesus. Those who flatly deny that it took place quickly find themselves on the back foot. Here are some of the rapid-fire questions they have to answer:

- If the resurrection did not take place, what happened to the body of Jesus? Why wasn't it found?
- Why did so many people claim to have seen the resurrected Jesus?
- The disciples died (as in, were executed) for their insistence that Jesus rose from the dead. They claimed they had encountered the risen Christ. If they knew they were lying, why didn't some of them (or all of them) change their story when they realized it would cost them their lives?
- How do you explain the dramatic change in the disciples after the claim of the resurrection of Jesus? It seems clear that something dramatic happened. If it wasn't the resurrection, what was it?

Or we could put the last point above a little differently:

- We know the disciples went on to change the world. That much is history. If it wasn't the resurrection, what was it that inspired this small group of fishermen to transform the world?

And so we could go on.

As you listen to the evidence, perhaps you sometimes find one argument convincing, then another seems more persuasive. The scales might tip for a while in the direction of belief, at other times not.

In the next section we shift our focus and ask about the impact of Christianity on world history. This is a fairly pragmatic test. Arguments about a necessary first cause can sound essentially theoretical. But if God is real, we would expect to find evidence of the fingerprints of God in the flow of history – ways in which believing in this God has made a difference, for good or for ill. If for ill, it could be that this God is not worth believing in, a force to be resisted rather than embraced. But if for good, we must be willing to note that the God hypothesis has had an essentially positive outcome. And surely that counts for something?

Let's explore the impact of the Christian faith on history.

Section B

But Faith is Morally Suspect

5

So Here's the Problem: Faith is Morally Suspect

At various points in this book you will have noticed my claim that Christianity has changed the world.

You could hear the claim with a sense of delight, and affirmatively reply, 'Yes, isn't it wonderful that the message of Jesus has done so much good.' But I am conscious that others will respond, 'Changed the world. Indeed it has. It has so much evil to answer for, so much blood on its hands.'

I tell this story at the start of my book *When Faith Turns Ugly*:[1]

It was an unexpected encounter at an art gallery and it left me unsettled and concerned. Rosemary and I had been admiring the entries for the Mandorla Art Award, and were impressed by the wide array of interpretations given to its 2014 theme, 'Elijah Meets God'. One of the viewers did not share our enthusiasm, and started to mutter angrily to me, 'How can they allow an exhibition like this? Don't they know anything about the Bible? It is such a bloodthirsty book. And how can they have a competition about Elijah? He killed off all his religious opponents. Religion, that's the problem with the world today, and now they're trying to sanitize it with this art award.'

I tried to present an alternative point of view, but he would have none of it. He appeared to be an ethically sensitive person, but at the deepest level of his being he seemed to find the idea of religion offensive. I wondered if he might feel a little differently about Jesus, as many people separate their views of institutionalized faith from their feelings about

Christ, but he turned out to be as vigorous an opponent of Jesus as he was of Elijah. 'Clearly you have never really examined his claims,' he told me. 'Fancy announcing that you are the only way, truth and life and that no one can get to God except through you. It's the breeding ground of intolerance, and look at the harvest of religious wars it has reaped.'

Again, my attempts to defend Jesus got nowhere. He left the gallery shortly afterwards, clearly annoyed that he had stumbled into a display that so offended his ethical sensibilities.

I have been a follower of Jesus for over forty years. During that time I have often encountered people who have expressed intellectual reservations about the trustworthiness of the Christian faith. As both a student and a teacher of apologetics, I have grappled with their questions and have, at least to my own satisfaction, resolved the majority of them. The remainder I have learnt to live with. They don't seem too significant to me. More recently, however, I have noticed a different tone to the objections. People seem a little less interested in debating whether miracles can or cannot happen, or if the Bible can or cannot be trusted. Their issue is not primarily with the question of truth, but with the question of moral credibility.

It has taken me by surprise, and I have spent the last few years wrestling with some of the issues raised. To me it has always seemed a self-evident truth that Christianity is a force for good in the world. I have seen so many faith-based projects bring light and hope to otherwise bleak and depressing landscapes. And I have met so many wonderful people whose faith in Jesus has touched and shaped them in such a way that their kindness and goodness spontaneously overflow into the lives of all who come into contact with them. I struggle to understand why people would question their integrity and morality – or the worthiness of the faith that has led to this transformation.

Perhaps it has been the many financial scandals in which the church has become embroiled. And then there are the heartbreaking cases of sexual abuse by the clergy – so many of them . . . And then there are the many examples of the abuse of power by religious leaders. If money, sex and power are the three false gods of our age, the church at times has been guilty of bowing down to each. The consequences are increasingly apparent. A watching world no longer believes that Christian leaders can be trusted, or that they have anything to contribute to the resolution of the ethical issues of our age. Faith is increasingly marginalized to a purely private zone, its presence in the public arena distrusted, unwelcome and often forbidden. How has it come to this?

The book goes on to examine what I believe is an essentially self-apparent truth, that while most versions of the Christian faith are life serving, a few are toxic, and it suggests ways to ensure that we embrace life-serving versions of faith.

All this is to acknowledge that as we look at the story of the impact of Christianity, there are at least two tales to be told. We should not attempt to whitewash our understanding of history, cherry-picking those happy moments of moral breakthrough and claiming Christianity as an unqualified force for good in the world.

Those who find it impossible to embrace faith are very conscious of the shadow side of Christianity, and if we are to ask if Christianity is probably true, we must listen to the full force of their argument. And we must ask them to be willing to consider the other side as well.

As we listen to both sides, we must not fall into the common trap that assumes that because a story has two sides, both are of equal weight. It is possible to consider something to be less than it could have been, even to have been deeply flawed in some aspects, and yet to be essentially good. Likewise the reverse can be true. Something may on the surface have many pleasing features, but if you were to dig a little deeper you might conclude that its overall impact is oppressive and to be actively resisted.

Let us then first hear the case against faith: the ugly side of the role of religion in history.

Why faith is inevitably a bad news story

There are those who believe that faith is inevitably a bad news story. While they would acknowledge that its cracks can be papered over, and that an outward veneer of good works and service to the community can give a superficial appearance of good, this simply hides the darker side of religion: its essential intolerance, its selective use of facts, and its fundamental commitment to otherworldly rather than this-worldly concerns.

For evidence, they do not have to look far. Stark reminders of the atrocities committed by Islamic fundamentalists surround us and are rapidly increasing. Christianity has a past that is less than squeaky clean – the Crusades, the Inquisition, and the bloodshed between Catholics and Protestants in Northern Ireland being a few of all too many possible examples. Other faiths fare no better. Hinduism with its belief in reincarnation instinctively buttresses the status quo, as it proclaims that a person's present life status is the valid outworking of karma accumulated in previous lifetimes. Buddhism is as bad; objectively viewed, it seems little more than a flight from reality – a refusal to attach significance to anything, the ultimate form of escapism.

Let's dig a little deeper into this. The objection at this point is that even if belief in God was entirely warranted, the outcome would be morally oppressive. In broad brush strokes, here are the key points that those who reject the moral value of religion usually make:

1. By appealing to otherworldly sources of authority (such as a book alleged to be divinely inspired) and claiming those sources to be infallible, religious people exempt themselves from wrestling with new evidence which might challenge their understanding. They simply declare it invalid, demonic or impossible. Examples abound. The church initially rejected all suggestions that the earth revolved around the sun, because this appeared to contradict the psalmist's observation that 'He set the earth on its foundations; it can never be moved' (Psalm 104:5). While theologians are now happy to view this passage as using a little poetic licence, they were remarkably slow to come to this point of view, and scientists such as Nicolaus Copernicus suffered grave injustices as a result.

   This inherent conservativism puts a brake on progress. It means that something other than a dispassionate exploration of the facts drives our agenda, and we therefore settle for second-rate decisions.

At its worst, it is much more serious. Wars have been waged in the name of God, and because divine authority for the war is claimed, its legitimacy cannot be challenged, making ordinary people pawns in the process. Further, if a war is seen to be authorized by God, there is little accountability for how the enemy is treated, for if God is on our side we need waste no time agonizing over the plight of the other. Take God out of the picture, and a more realistic assessment of the conflict is likely: 'We are at war with this country because it threatens our national interest' is more honest than 'We are in a divinely mandated conflict (perhaps a jihad) and are therefore unquestionably in the right'.

2. The world's major faiths were birthed during the long patriarchal period of history and are unable to move beyond this. They are therefore trapped by gender stereotypes and uphold views of the world that are oppressive towards women and minority groups, such as the LGBTI community. They attempt to justify the unjustifiable in the name of God, thinking that the appeal to God should excuse their views from serious scrutiny. The most senior religious leaders are almost all male, and most religions have a narrative that ensures that this is likely to continue for the foreseeable future. Put differently, no one is predicting a female pope any time soon.

3. Because people want their religion to be true, they filter out all arguments against it. They become uncritical supporters of their faith and abandon the rationality they usually show in other areas of life. It is all too easy to find ways to rationalize evidence against God. So, for example, while Christians proclaim that God is love, if a terrible disaster takes place and people suffer greatly as a result, Christians often claim that there is some wider plan at work and that while we may not see the purpose now, we will in time. Cynics note that this is simply a way of allowing nothing – not even compelling evidence – to count against a prior faith-based conviction. If nothing is allowed to count against a belief, it is inherently unfalsifiable. While the holder of the belief might find this convincing, outsiders view it as reframing evidence to suit an unquestioning allegiance.

4. Religion makes people intolerant. It is worse than nationalism, because while nationalism's only claim to legitimacy is 'You were born here; you owe us', religion pretends to be true. Religious people feel entitled to judge and moralize about the evils of others, because they believe that they alone have the key to truth. They therefore instinctively distrust those outside their faith, because they believe those people have not yet found the truth. Many religions have an evangelical component where followers try to reach out to those who do not believe as they do, but this often becomes ugly, with people being required to renounce what they once held dear when they are converted.

5. Religion makes us search for solutions outside ourselves. It is like whistling in the dark. It hopes for an outside saviour, and so does not take seriously the human mandate to secure the future of this planet. It urges us to wait for God instead of getting us to assume responsibility for our own destiny. People pray, and so presume that someone else (God) will assume responsibility, instead of fostering the enormous creativity that lies within all human communities. It therefore makes no real contribution to the progress of this planet.

6. Religion plays to the fear that exists inside most people, especially the fear of death. Most religions threaten dire consequences for those who reject their teaching, sometimes even threatening eternal torment. Many are terrified into conversion, while others make a token commitment to a particular faith – often as a way to hedge their bets. While supposed to offer comfort to the bereaved, when logically thought through, many religions add to the burden of bereavement by suggesting that if the person who has died was not of that faith, he or she now faces eternal punishment. Clearly this exacerbates an already traumatic situation. One could even go further, and suggest that religion is a bully, spotting the vulnerabilities in others and playing on them for its own advantage.

7. Religion fosters fake morality. While religious people often engage in charitable acts, their motivation is usually to please their God or to fulfil a religious obligation. Their action is therefore essentially

extrinsic to their being and not a reflection of their inner world. Religious people do good things because there is something in it for them, for they believe their actions make them more pleasing to their God. Put differently, religion fosters external forms of morality, rather than intrinsic morality which flows from the actual nature of the person. Charitable religious acts are about appearances rather than a benevolent inner world. Despite its claims to transform people, religion does not lead to inner transformation but only to external outer conformity to the norms of the particular faith. Sometimes this expresses itself in even more distressing forms, as for example when religious groups provide needed aid to an impoverished community but in return require that the community convert to the religion or face the termination of the aid.

While this list is not exhaustive, and you might be adding an eighth or ninth point, it gives a sense of the kinds of concerns held by those who reject faith. These concerns should not be trivialized. Those of us who have embraced faith have usually done so not only because we believe that God is real, but also out of a conviction that our faith is good not only for us but for the world. And most of us long not just for a glorious afterlife but also a better world in the here and now. If religion is unlikely to lead to this, it is indeed a serious argument against faith.

And there have been more than a few troubling abuses of faith. Is religion poisonous? Is its inevitable outcome religious wars and the like?

At times the answer has been 'yes'. It is difficult to pretend that the Crusades were unrelated to the Christian faith that inspired, motivated and seemed to justify those bloodthirsty campaigns. To try to sidestep responsibility for this is foolish. And lest we think that such atrocities are confined to a long past era, it is confronting to realize that in the Rwandan civil war (1990–94), Hutu preachers regularly cited King Saul's failure to heed God's instruction in 1 Samuel 15 to utterly destroy the Amalekites, including their children, infants and cattle, and warned that the Hutus would face a similar rejection by God if they failed to totally destroy their Tutsi neighbours. Their congregations were all too obedient. Philip Jenkins comments sadly and resignedly on this tragic misapplication of Scripture: 'The last Christian who will seek to exterminate another nation on the pretence of killing Amalekites has not yet been born.'[2]

Sadly, I could keep on giving examples of the misuse of faith. And it usually is the misuse of faith that is the issue. In other words, it is not faith itself that is the cause of the abuse, but faith being used to achieve another end. In the Rwandan example above, the issue was not religion as such, but the way it was used to manipulate and conscript people into serving the national and political aspirations of local power-holders. Much the same can be said of multiple other atrocities where religion is blamed but was primarily used as a foil for the illegitimate goals of those who knew how to 'play' the religious card. For all that, the consequences have sometimes been so serious that we cannot view this argument as a get-out-of-jail-free card and act as though it excuses everything.

But is the picture presented above definitive and fair?

Let's turn our attention to the opposite point of view, that religion is a force for good. Actually, as the thesis of this book is that Christianity is probably true, the focus will be crisper: we will start by asking whether Christianity has primarily been a force for good or evil in its history and then mull over the implications of the answer.

Realistically, if Christianity has done more harm than good, it is probably not true, or if true, it is clearly mistaken in the notion that its God is loving and sent his Son Jesus into the world that we might have 'life, and have it to the full' – a claim the Bible records Jesus making in John 10:10.

On the other hand, if Christianity has been a force for good, and especially if it has been a significant force for good, this strengthens (though does not decisively prove) the argument that Christianity is probably true.

Let's explore the evidence . . .

6

But Have You Considered? Not Such a Shabby History

Perhaps you were taken aback by the last chapter. The case against faith sounded strong, and the argument that it is essentially morally suspect may well have convinced you. But here's the thing: while at a theoretical level you can look at the accusations – faith removes your objectivity, makes you complacently accept the unacceptable, takes away the ability to question, and the like – the actual experience of the Christian faith in human history tells a rather different story. And ironically, the most tragic tale of all has been woven not by those who claim religious faith but by those who renounced it, as is made abundantly clear by the absolutely appalling harvest of human lives and suffering in countries dominated by atheistic communism during the twentieth century.

For a moment let's forget about what we think religious faith should or should not achieve in the world, and consider what it actually has achieved. If the proof of the pudding is in the eating, this is a pretty pragmatic test, where the rubber hits the road (to use another metaphor). Does faith work?

My focus in this chapter will be on the Christian faith, and at a later point I will explain why. The question we're considering is simple and focused: has Christianity done more good than harm? It is followed by a related question: is it a close call, or does the evidence point overwhelmingly (though not necessarily exclusively) in one direction?

The church: hazard or witness?

When you hear the word 'church' are you more inclined to think, 'Now that's why I can't believe' or 'Yep, it sure is another of those niggling little signs that God's hand has been at work and that belief in God is warranted'? Given the bad press the church has experienced in recent years, I imagine that many will select the former. Some will boldly say that the church is hazardous and exposure to it is likely to leave you less inclined to believe in the existence of a good God. But I'd like to suggest that such thinking is blinkered and biased, and that deeper reflection on the question is more likely to lead to faith than to cynicism.

Why?

First let's face the bad news. Why is the Christian faith, and more particularly the Christian church, currently viewed with deep suspicion? Ten common accusations against the Christian faith, in no particular order, are its complicity in:

1. Religious warfare
2. Colonial exploitation
3. Racial bigotry
4. The subjugation of women
5. Homophobia
6. The abuse of the environment
7. Retarding the progress of science, especially medical science
8. Academic censorship
9. Intolerance of anything new
10. Sexual abuse, especially of children

Clearly there is nothing attractive about this list, particularly as it finds further support in David Kinnaman and Gabe Lyons' study of the attitude of 16–29-year-old Americans towards Christianity.[1] They note six recurring and unflattering images of Christians as:

1. Hypocritical
2. Interested in 'saving' people rather than in relating to them

3. Anti-homosexual
4. Sheltered
5. Too political
6. Judgmental

Again, the list is far from winsome. But lists are easy to draw up, especially if you have two thousand years of history to draw from. Furthermore, billions of people have claimed allegiance to the Christian faith, so it is easy to find a fair few who have done awful things.

Writing in his letter to the Galatians, the apostle Paul records perhaps the most revolutionary concept that had been expressed in human history until that point. In its own way it changed the world, for once you grasp its implications and attempt to live by them, a world of those who are in and those who are out, a world of the favoured and the excluded, is no longer possible. It is a portrait of the world where everyone matters, a logical extension of the belief that all human beings have been made in the image of God. In this passage Paul writes: 'There is neither Jew nor Gentile, neither slave nor free, neither male nor female, for you are all one in Christ Jesus' (Galatians 3:28 TNIV).

Written for the early Christian community, it outlines a manner of life among Christians which was to take little account of a person's nationality, social standing and gender. It was more than radical for the time; it was unheard of. That slaves and Gentiles and men and women and Jews and nobles could stand on level ground and relate as believers together . . . well, that's the kind of vision which, given enough time, changes the world. And indeed, that is what it did.

Countering the suggestion that the church should duck for cover when its record is surveyed, Alvin Schmidt in his book *Under the Influence: How Christianity Transformed Civilization*[2] reminds us of the astonishing contribution made by the church in the transformation of the world, and convincingly argues that without the influence of the church we would not have seen the various developments described below. (This is not his complete list, and I have supplemented it with the insights of some other authors.)

1. The sanctification of human life. Schmidt argues that the Christian belief that every person has been made in the image of God has led to the conviction that every human life is of immense value. This had already been picked up in Judaism during the period of history before Christ, a point of difference between the Jews and their pagan neighbours being the Jewish refusal to participate in child sacrifices. This was accelerated with the advent of Christianity, particularly because Christians believe that Jesus was God incarnate. If God took on human form, this validates the sacredness of human life at the deepest level. Consequently, early Christians, shocked by the low value attached to life in the Roman Empire, opposed infanticide, infant abandonment, abortion and the gladiatorial games.

Infanticide, which was commended by, among others, Plato, Aristotle, Cicero and Seneca, was a legitimate state policy in Rome, reflected the teaching found in the Twelve Tables, the earliest known Roman legal code (c.450 BCE). It permitted fathers to expose their female infants or deformed or weak male infants to the elements. Naturally the vast majority of these babies did not survive the ordeal.[3] So widespread was the practice that Polybius (c.205–118 BCE) blamed it for the population decline in ancient Greece. Infant girls were especially vulnerable, to the extent that it was extremely rare in ancient Greece for wealthy families to raise more than one daughter. A second-century inscription found in Delphi indicates that out of six hundred families, only 1% had raised two daughters.[4]

The low value attached to life was also underlined by the popularity of the gladiator games, which were commonplace for over three hundred years. Most gladiators were slaves, criminals or prisoners of war, and were considered to be without worth or humanity. Trained to fight to the death in the arena, often against other gladiators, but sometimes against starved wild beasts, hundreds of thousands of gladiators were mauled, mangled and gored to death. Their lives were considered to not matter at all. These games were stopped after Christianity became the religion of the empire – a direct consequence of the very different value now attached to human life. Schmidt makes a valid point when he writes: 'People who today see murder and mass atrocities as immoral may not realize that their beliefs in this regard are largely the result of their having internalized the Christian ethic that holds human life to be sacred.'[5] This is a telling point. We have indeed become so accustomed to attaching value to human life that we assume it is automatic. History tells a different story, and points to a decisive shift occurring with the advent of Christianity.

2. The elevation of sexual morality. The world in which the early church found itself was highly promiscuous. The Christian contention that sex should be an expression of mutual love and respect, and that it should only be practised within marriage, was seen as radical. This was a time when paedophilia, incest and bestiality were widely practised and condoned. While critics rightly denounce the church every time it violates its own code of sexual ethics, they sometimes forget that it was the church that was instrumental in outlawing practices such as paedophilia.

The irony in this should not be missed. As the originator of a strong code of sexual ethics, particularly a code that protects children, the church is without excuse when it fails to uphold its own teaching. But do not overlook the fact that the Romans considered paedophilia a normal part of everyday life. It was because of the rise of Christianity that this changed, and those of any faith or none should acknowledge their indebtedness to Christianity for this.

3. The championing of the rights of women. We have noted how radical Paul's sentiment in Galatians 3:28 is, that in Christ 'there is neither Jew nor Gentile, neither slave nor free, neither male nor female, for you are all one in Christ Jesus'. Even a cursory glance at the status of women in countries deeply impacted by the Christian faith, as opposed to those where the impact has been slight, reveals an obvious difference. We have already noted that the infanticide rate of female babies in ancient Greece and Rome was dramatically higher than that of males, a reflection of the low value attached to the birth of a baby girl. While a husband could divorce his wife, a wife could not divorce her husband. Table Four of the Twelve Tables of Rome spelled out the law of *patria potestas*, which conferred the right of *paterfamilias* on the married man, giving him absolute power over both his wife and children. He could kill his wife for adultery, and, for an offence considered less serious than adultery, could murder her with the consent of the extended family. While this right was rarely implemented, its mere existence ensured that women thought very carefully before they expressed an independent or dissenting voice. Women were without rights and freedoms. Child brides were common, and often only 11 or 12 years of age.

Given this context, the attitude of Jesus to women was stunning. He showed them respect, spent time teaching Mary at her home and commended her willingness to learn to Martha (a strong contrast to the view expressed in the Jewish *Sotah* 3:4: 'Let the words of the Torah be burned rather than taught to women'), and he selected women to be the first witnesses of the empty tomb and thus bearers of the most significant news ever delivered to the human race. (This is one of several reasons why the resurrection accounts should be believed; no one would have fabricated a story in which women were the first witnesses, as the general response would have been 'We're supposed to believe that because a woman saw it!') Today we sometimes accuse the church of holding women back. In the opening centuries of Christianity the exact opposite accusation would have been made – that the church failed to keep women in their place, or what was considered to be their place in Rome.

The impact of Christianity can be clearly seen when in 374 CE the Roman emperor Valentinian I, moved by the example of Christ and the teaching of the apostle Paul, revoked the *patria potestas*. Note the significance of this. Within roughly half a century of the legalization of Christianity, this still newish faith was dramatically transforming society for the better by revoking laws that had stood for almost a thousand years and had legitimized the oppression of women throughout the Roman Empire.

4. The birth of charity and compassion. We take the parable of the Good Samaritan so much for granted that we have forgotten that its teaching was not self-evident in its time, and even less so in the broader context of the Greco-Roman world of Jesus' day. Helping others in need, especially those who were not part of your family or clan, was a genuinely novel idea. The early Christians practised *caritas* – what we would call 'charity' – that is, giving to relieve the plight of another without any expectation of the gift being returned. By contrast, the Romans practised *liberalitas* – gift giving to the privileged to please them in the hope that they would later bestow a favour on the giver. There was no instinctive drive to help the needy. Plato (427–347 BCE) advised that a poor person no longer able to work should be left to die. The Roman philosopher Plautus (254–184 BCE) wrote: 'You do a beggar bad service by giving him food and drink; you lose what you give and prolong his life for more misery.'[6] Reflecting upon this Schmidt writes: 'When modern secularists show compassion today upon seeing or hearing of some human tragedy . . . they show that they have unknowingly internalized Christianity's concept of compassion . . . [if they had not] grown up under the two-thousand-year-old umbrella of Christianity's compassionate influence, they would probably be without much compassion, similar to the ancient Greeks, Romans, and others.'[7]

5. Development of hospitals and health care. Jesus was both a teacher and a healer. When he sent his disciples out on their first mission, they were entrusted with a similar ministry, Luke 9:2 informing us that they were to preach the kingdom of God and heal those who were ill. Christianity has always had a special concern for the sick. Perhaps understandably, most people in Roman society viewed the sick with contempt and fear, anxious lest they too be struck down by the malady that had befallen the ill person. Howard Haggard has noted that 'When epidemics broke out [the Romans] often fled in fear and left the sick to die without a care'.[8] Generally the Romans viewed compassion as a sign of weakness. It was Christianity that transformed this, showing it to be a sign not of weakness but of strength.

It is true that the Greeks had shrines where the sick could go in hope of healing, and also had the *iatreia*, which some see as the forerunner of the modern hospital system. However, these were simply places where ill people went to have their ailments diagnosed by the physicians of the day, and to have medicines prescribed for them. No nursing or ongoing care was provided. The Romans had the *valetudinaria*, but these buildings were primarily for the care of Roman soldiers or gladiators, and were not accessible to the common people, who had no place of refuge in time of need. It is noteworthy that at the very first ecumenical council of the church, held in Nicaea in 325, the bishops directed that a hospice be built in every city that had a cathedral. These facilities were not limited to caring for the sick, but also had to provide shelter for the poor and lodging for pilgrims. Again, note how quickly this occurred after the legitimization of the Christian faith. Once legal, Christians immediately set about transforming society for good. This has been for the benefit not just of Christians but of the world.

6. The opening of education. If the formation of hospitals was in response to Jesus' compassion and ministry to the sick, the widening and opening of education to all was a response to his role as a teacher. To be sure, Christianity was not the first faith to be involved in education, but, because of the great value it placed on all people, it dramatically broadened the brief as to who should be educated. The Romans and Greeks taught those from wealthy backgrounds. With only a few exceptions, those educated were men. It was Christianity that first educated both sexes together. The fruit of this was quickly apparent, Augustine in the fifth century noting that Christian women were often better informed in their faith than pagan male philosophers.[9] This is not to suggest that the cathedral schools which existed from the fourth to the tenth century taught boys and girls in equal numbers, for the number of boys educated was unquestionably higher than girls, but in spite of this, Christianity was opening doors for women that had never previously been opened. Well-educated women started to feature as thought leaders during the Middle Ages with a frequency unknown in prior human history. Nunneries educated girls in the liberal arts. Some went on to become nuns, often making significant contributions to their order, while others became important leaders in their own field.

After the Protestant Reformation, the concern for education accelerated. While today we think of Sunday school as a place for children to learn about the Christian faith, the original Sunday schools were set up to educate children (and sometimes adults) from impoverished homes who were working on every other day of the week. For many of these children, it empowered them to break out of the cycle of poverty and to reach their potential.[10]

I do not want to overemphasize the point, but in addition to Schmidt's list above we can add that Christianity has been closely linked to most of the progressive social developments in history. Greg Sheridan entitles chapter 3 of his book *God Is Good for You*, 'What did we ever get from Christianity – apart from the idea of the individual, human rights, feminism, liberalism, modernity, social justice and secular politics?', and the chapter goes on to vigorously defend this enormous claim.[11] You cannot study the abolition of slavery without telling the story of William Wilberforce and pointing back to his strong Christian faith and his conviction that this was the path God had led him on. Likewise you cannot study the rise of labour movements around the world without noting the theological convictions of most of its champions, and their sense that they were compelled by God to work for economic protection and safeguards for workers around the world. Imagine how much poorer the world would be if core Christian beliefs had not found their logical outworking in the way in which we order society and protect those who are the most vulnerable.

Let me, however, explore one more important link, that of the relationship between progress in science and Christianity, if only because so many falsely believe that science and Christianity must be enemies. History tells a different story. True, we have noted the unacceptable treatment of Copernicus because of his discovery that the earth and planets revolve around the sun, but a focus on such stories (and there are others) misses a much broader point.

Unlike followers of pagan religions, Christians have always believed in a rational God, who is distinct from the creation. People, as image bearers of this rational God, are also called to be rational and to follow logic where it leads. To some extent Aristotle also championed this, but Aristotelian philosophy was essentially deductive, focusing on what could be systematically reasoned in the realm of the mind. It was not inductive – testing ideas in the realm of reality. Furthermore, the undergirding worldview was pantheistic, seeing the gods and nature as intertwined. Thus it was believed that the planets moved because of their own inner intelligence which caused them to move. This is significant as it delayed the advancement of science, because you cannot experiment on stones or shrubs if you believe they have the spirits of various gods or ancestors living inside them. The Christian insistence on a God distinct from the creation removed this obstacle.

We should not undervalue the importance this had in the development of science. Until well into the eighteenth century almost every notable scientist attributed whatever insight they had gained to their belief in God, and they were correct, for the reason they embarked on the scientific enterprise was their deep conviction that there were scientific laws waiting to be discovered because there was a lawgiver, God, who had put these laws into place. It was actually deeper than this. They believed that God had created a rational universe according to the laws of nature, and these laws were waiting to be discovered by those who had been created in God's own image, and who had been entrusted with the task of being stewards of creation, as taught in Genesis 1:27–28 and Genesis 2:19–20. Once this conviction gained traction, science advanced rapidly. Name the scientific greats: Roger Bacon (1214–94), Johann Kepler (1571–1630), Galileo (1564–1642), Robert Boyle (1627–91), Isaac Newton (1642–1727), André Ampere (1775–1836), Michael Faraday (1791–1867), Louis Pasteur (1822–95), Joseph Lister (1827–1912). Each of them helped to advance our planet greatly, and each set about their work with the firm conviction that the Christian God had created a rational world. Because they believed in a lawgiver, they believed there were laws waiting to be discovered. This firm conviction did not disappoint them. Indeed, they considered it vindicated as they made breakthrough after breakthrough.

When next you hear someone thoughtlessly say, 'Science and Christianity contradict each other', think through this list of greats (and I could have added so many others) and remember that each one of them would shake their head at the comment and reply, 'I must strongly disagree.'

There is a reason why those countries most impacted by the Christian faith soared ahead of others when it came to scientific progress. It was not that their citizens were brighter, for that is simply not true. It was that they operated from a different view of the world. It was a view that affirmed that God was the first cause of the universe – a creator distinct from the creation, a creator who had put in place laws which govern the universe and which are capable of being discovered by those who bear the image of this God. It is a view of reality which has been enormously fruitful.

Could the fruitfulness be because these views of God are true?

This is not an idea to be sneered at. Rather it must be taken with the utmost seriousness. If we work from certain assumptions and the result of working from those assumptions is very fruitful, we usually assume that the assumptions are correct. This is one of many reasons why it is perfectly rational to conclude that Christianity is probably true; after all, it works in practice, and that should not be taken lightly.

Where have we got to in this discussion?

The bottom line is this: has Christianity, and the Christian church in particular, always got things right? No. But it has got them more right than any other significant group, and that by more than a little bit. There are no close challengers. The world would be inconceivably worse off without the gift of the Christian faith and the church it has birthed. Imperfect though the church is, it is another niggling little sign that there is a God working in the world and doing so for its good.

Is Christianity past its use-by date?

You may have found yourself largely in agreement with the previous section but remain unconvinced that the overall thesis that God probably exists has been strengthened by these insights. Although you may struggle to put your objection into words, it is possible that you feel that while the overall contribution of Christianity to the world has been positive, a different era now lies ahead of us, and that new challenges require fresh thinking, uncluttered by the restrictions of the past. Put differently, you may be trying to find a polite way to suggest that Christianity is well beyond its use-by date.

Perhaps you feel more strongly than this. Some argue that in spite of a valuable opening contribution to the progress of this planet, Christianity now acts as a brake on moral progress. To support this, they point to what they would consider to be the inflexibility of Christian thought on issues such as gender, sexuality, global warming, the beginning and end of life, genetic engineering, the usefulness of artificial intelligence, and the willingness to seriously explore the origin of life or the quest to find life on other planets.

The assumption appears to be that while previously Christianity was committed to the quest for truth, it now wishes to impose a moratorium on creative thought and to allow little more than tinkering around the edges of what already is. In the media, it is far more common for a Christian leader to be quoted for their opposition to some new development than for their support of it. The faith seems to have become inherently conservative, very quick to object to changes in society. Have Christians been reduced to a set of naysayers?

A reality check is in order at this point.

Given that Christianity is the world's largest religion, it is very difficult to speak of the Christian view on any particular issue with the conviction that all 2 billion of its adherents will quickly nod in agreement. Christianity has many different tribes, and the answer you get on an issue often depends on who you are talking to. Do Christians believe that women can be ordained as clergy? Depends on which Christians you talk to. Do Christians believe in evolution? Depends on which Christians you talk to. Do Christians support gay marriage? Depends on which Christians you talk to. And so I could go on.

True, the proportion of Christians agreeing or disagreeing on any issue would differ greatly, so if your approach was one of 'winner takes all', you might quickly silence some of the more colourful voices on the fringes of Christianity. History would warn us of the folly of such an approach. Don't forget that while William Wilberforce was strongly motivated by his Christian faith to work for the abolition of slavery, he faced the strong opposition of many sincere Christians who believed that they found a mandate for slavery in the Bible, especially in the Old Testament. That is not an isolated example.

This is a genuinely complex issue and one which we must not gloss over too quickly.

Part of the success of Christianity has been its ability to adapt to changing times and cultures. Not only is it a very old religion; it is also the world's most widespread faith. Sometimes it has caught the imagination of an entire culture and been an important influence in shaping its future. At other times the impact has been less, and it has been embraced by only small pockets within the community. Nevertheless, there are very few societies where Christianity is completely voiceless. Its ability to penetrate and impact diverse thought-forms has been truly remarkable. Perhaps we could even see it as another of those niggling little suggestions that this faith is probably true, for of all the faiths in the world, it seems to be the only one able to find an opening in almost any setting.

The real test is whether the Christian faith is sufficiently robust to continue to be a force for good in a world which has already embraced many Christian values, such as the need to care for one's neighbour, but now wishes to progress further in the moral quest. Does Christianity still have something to offer?

It depends on which version of the Christian faith you look at. Being as large as it is, it is hardly surprising that forms of faith have emerged that bear little resemblance to the original message of Jesus. Jesus had many harsh words to say to the religious leaders of his day, and I imagine that he will have some comparably harsh words to say to some who claim to follow him today. He actually predicted that this would be the case, announcing in Matthew 7:21–23 that not all who say 'Lord, Lord' will enter the kingdom of heaven. In other words, Jesus encouraged us not to uncritically embrace everything that claims to be Christian but rather to test it to see if it accords with his own teaching.

In proposing that Christianity is probably true, I am not suggesting that everything that has the name 'Christian' attached to it should be defended and viewed as strengthening the hypothesis. Some forms of the Christian faith are simply unhelpful, and we should never attempt to defend the indefensible.

Fundamentalism, for example, is a version of faith that Jesus would almost certainly have rejected. Its rigidity and instinctive intolerance reflects a very different attitude from the one displayed by Jesus when he walked through the villages and towns of Galilee. It appeals to people who are easily threatened by others and who long to be in control of situations by having all rules agreed in advance. It was the fundamentalism of the religious leaders of Jesus' day that saw them threatened by his message, and unable to celebrate the new and profound insights he announced. Think for example of how deeply offended they were that Jesus performed miracles on the Sabbath day. His actions undermined their strict code of what could and could not happen on the Sabbath, thereby making them feel a little less in control of the process. So trapped were they within their little systems that they found themselves unable to celebrate the miracles that took place on the Sabbath, such as that a man who had been blind from birth was able to see (John 9) and that another who had been lame for thirty-eight years was suddenly able to walk (John 5).

Fundamentalism is an old trap, and is every bit as damaging today as it was in Jesus' day. Jesus' own condemnation of it in Matthew 23 is worth pondering, especially his warning that we should not neglect 'the more important matters of the law – justice, mercy and faithfulness' (Matthew 23:23).

Rather than settle for noting what should be avoided, let me make a positive plea for what we should look out for and encourage.

In my opinion, versions of the Christian faith that will continue to make a real contribution to the well-being of this planet will be characterized by their fidelity to the three important 'orthos' of the faith – orthodoxy, orthopraxy and orthopathy. What do I mean by these?

Orthodoxy is about right belief, remaining true to orthodox understandings of the Christian faith throughout the centuries. These have been summarized in a few of the creeds of Christianity, including the Nicene Creed and the Apostles' Creed. They reflect the broad themes found in the Bible. Orthodoxy does not have to be rigid; it can have a generous flexibility which allows treasured truths of the faith to be viewed from slightly different angles. But it still defers back to orthodox understandings of the faith, helping to deepen our insight into what has been traditionally held, rather than causing us to renounce what has been previously believed.

Orthodoxy on its own can seem cold and sterile – right belief divorced from life. This is why the other two orthos are also important.

Orthopraxy is about right practice. It means putting love into action. Orthopraxy quietly insists that any version of the Christian faith that is content with one talkfest after another, without words being translated into a fruitful and compassionate way of life, is inadequate.

Orthopathy takes this one step further. It is about right feeling. It is possible to both believe the right thing and do the right thing, but to do so without genuine empathy or care. Cold charity, like cold orthodoxy, is . . . cold. A good example of a lack of orthopathy is implied in Jesus' parable of the prodigal son, found in Luke 15:11–32. While you initially think that the parable is about the son who made an early claim on his father's estate and squandered the money he gained on prostitutes and wild living, the story is wonderfully nuanced. It also tells of an older stay-at-home brother, and it turns out that this man was every bit as much of an important character as his younger sibling. This older brother has always done the right thing and worked hard for his father, but when his younger brother returns home, penniless and dejected (but having learnt a great deal about true and false love), the older man refuses to join the celebrations to mark the return. He is reprimanded by his father for his attitude, for though the older son believed and did the right things, there was something profoundly wrong with his heart. He had no empathy for his younger brother, and that meant that even though he believed and did the right things, he fell far short of the mark. Orthopathy matters, for genuine versions of the Christian faith call us to feel *with* others, and to be as quick to sense what their worlds are like as we do our own.

If this trio harmonize together – orthodoxy, with orthopraxy, with orthopathy – they combine to be a powerful force for good.

I should single out one more aspect that seems to me to be crucial in ensuring that Christianity continues to shape our world for the good. It revolves around good theology, and understanding the initial mandate given to humanity at the creation of the world.

In the opening chapter of the Bible we are told that both men and women were created in the image of God. Genesis 2 elaborates on this by giving a quick snapshot of one of Adam's earliest tasks. It is the sort of task that only an image bearer could do, for it involved great creativity and insight. In a world where the animals and birds had not yet been named, God assigned the responsibility of name allocation to Adam, watching as the human made his decisions.

Now I realize that some of my readers will be switching off at this point, doing so after objecting, 'You can't possibly expect me to continue reading if you insist on speaking of the Adam and Eve story as though it actually happened.' Let me push back. Regardless of whether you read Genesis 1 – 3 as history, or as a theological commentary on how to understand the origin and purpose of the world, your conclusions on the intentions behind these chapters are likely to be the same. So if you reject the historicity of Genesis 1 – 3, keep reading . . . and if you accept its historicity, keep reading!

The portrait of Adam assuming responsibility for the naming of the birds and animals is stunning. Names help to shape the one named. In allocating to Adam the responsibility to name animals and birds, God is essentially saying, 'I made them; now you shape what they will become.' The fact that God is content to act as an onlooker while Adam performs this key task shows how seriously God views the human contribution to world shaping. The passage essentially invites us to conclude that humans are called to build a world with a better name – but to do so with the awareness that God is watching as we do. God may not quickly override our decisions, but we are ultimately responsible to God for the names we confer and the world we build.

It does not take too much imagination to sense the far-reaching implications of this. At a time when technological advances make previously unimagined versions of life possible, the mandate to build a world with a better name remains. It will not always be easy to predict the exact outcome of every twist or turn, but even a perfunctory grasp of this passage challenges us to risk new possibilities. Adam was not given the option of leaving things as they were. He had to concretely engage with the ongoing development of what God had created – and so must we.

We could add one further insight to this. In his letter to the Ephesians Paul reflects on the new church that is being birthed – a church now made up of both Jews and Gentiles, as the old divisions in society simply melted away in the light of the story of Jesus. He notes that this new community is 'built on the foundation of the apostles and prophets, with Christ Jesus himself as the chief cornerstone' (Ephesians 2:20). The different building blocks for faith that Paul enumerates are important. They are the apostles, the prophets, and Christ Jesus as cornerstone. Put differently, the convictions and beliefs of this new community were being shaped by the teaching of the apostles, who had at first hand observed the life of Jesus, and were now actively engaged in the task of planting the church in a hostile environment and were learning much from their new experiences. They were also shaped by the prophets, or the teaching from their Jewish past. This rich heritage continued to inform and guide them, though at times they reinterpreted what they had previously learnt and applied it in a very different way – their attitude to the Gentiles being one clear example of this. The insights from both the apostles and the prophets had to pass through another grid: that of the life and teaching of Jesus. Paul proclaims Christ Jesus to be the chief cornerstone. Every teaching, practice and attitude adopted by the church had to pass the Jesus test. Theologians today often talk of the necessity of reading the Bible with a Christological lens, and it is essentially this that they are referring to. No passage in the Bible, no experience from church history and no challenge in the present time should be evaluated outside the life and teaching of Jesus. It is the default drive through which everything must be assessed, and it provides a check against faulty understandings of the Christian faith that could otherwise arise.

As we set about the task of building a world with a better name, we should do so while constantly referring back to the attitudes, life, teaching and practice of Jesus. When we do so, we will notice what is blindingly obvious: Jesus was no reactionary conservative. He proclaimed a radical new order, one in which God, humanity and creation were reconciled and living together in rich harmony.

Is Christianity past its use-by date? It depends on how deeply we allow ourselves to be shaped by the life and teaching of Jesus. There is no reason to believe that those who accept this invitation will make any less of a contribution to the flourishing of this planet than their forebears did. This is a reason for people of any faith, or none, to be grateful. For genuine expressions of the Christian faith always work for good. It's one of the reasons that Christianity – in its Jesus-shaped form – is probably true.

Can you be a little more helpful? Or how do you spot a healthy church?

I'd like to close this chapter on a practical note. Some readers might be thinking that they'd love to be part of a church community that is genuinely helping to build a world with a better name. But how do you know which churches are doing this and which are not?

While it is unhelpful to be instinctively distrustful of local expressions of the church, it can be useful to look out for some signs that any particular church is being more or less successful in its attempt to follow Jesus.

Here are twelve signs that I encourage people to look out for. Don't dismiss a place because it doesn't get everything right, and perhaps you could help make up the shortfall in areas where it is not yet achieving. Whatever the case, look out for these signs of a healthy church.

1. **You sense that this is a place about God.** While I would like to think this sign is redundant, meeting with the reply, 'What else

would church be about?', my observation is that this is a sign you can't take for granted. It is so easy for church to become 'Church Inc.' – a smooth-running business that can manage, dare I say it, without God. Not that God isn't frequently referred to or acknowledged by the church members, but you just sense that God isn't really driving the agenda, that passion for God has waned, and that if God intends to do anything in the place it will have to be done on their terms. By contrast, the members of healthy churches have a sense of expectancy that overflows into spontaneous prayer, a tangible sense of dependence upon God, a willingness to risk and the courage to embrace projects that can only succeed if God is behind them.

2. **It is a place where people matter.** You quickly spot the cues that this is so. There is a gentleness that recognizes the vulnerability that is never far from the surface of any of us. There is often much humour, but the laughter that results is never the laughter of derision or from belittling others. Actually, there is a great deal of respect, and the stories that are told are stories that matter. They are stories that birth hope, and encourage us and inspire us to become a little more than we otherwise would be. Genuine conversations emerge. If it is a topic that touches life, it is a topic that gets talked about, and the discussion is honest and open and unafraid, and salted with care and concern for the other.

3. **Ethics matter.** While all churches must keep an eye on results and such matters as attendance, giving of time and money, and all those things that are needed if a church is to keep functioning, a healthy church is never deluded into thinking that the end always justifies the means. Healthy churches remember that the way we reach our targets and goals defines us. In a real sense the means become the end, and if the means we use are messy, we deceive ourselves if we think a healthy outcome will result. What does this mean in practice? Sometimes churches have to make difficult decisions. Not every ministry appointment works out, while some volunteers turn out to have an inflated sense of their ability (and don't we all struggle when someone who would like to sing in the worship team turns out to be painfully tuneless?). A healthy church

won't pull an ostrich stunt at that point and hope the problem will mysteriously disappear, but will deal with such issues respectfully, honestly, compassionately, creatively – yes, ethically.

4. **Worship matters.** Worship is far more than the songs we sing at a Sunday service and there are many ways in which we express our adoration of God, but in healthy churches there is something tangibly special about the way in which the congregation reaches out to God. When they gather, you sense the plus-one factor. It is the people gathered – plus God. Being gathered helps you to reach beyond yourself to connect with Jesus, who promised to be present where as few as two or three gather in his name (Matthew 18:20). In practical terms this means that when we sing, we sing; we don't see people fold their arms or roll their eyes because it's their least favourite song (again). When we pray, we pray, and our minds are turning to and tuning in to the God who hears and listens. When we listen to preaching, a healthy congregation does so with soft and expectant hearts. God may well have a word for us. Why not this week, when it has happened so often before?

5. **All ages matter.** Church is family. And healthy families embrace each generation. True, some programmes may focus on a particular age group, but you quickly realize this is not a church primarily for young people or old people or families or whatever subgroup we might target, but that all ages matter. Good families care for family members at all stages of life, and the church should reflect family life at its best.

6. **The Bible is a creative guide.** While this never means less-than-sound biblical teaching, it does mean more. It is possible to unpack biblical principles in an accurate but lifeless way. It is possible to speak about the Bible without any existential imagination, missing the way its ancient stories connect with today. Healthy churches have Bible teachers who live in both the biblical text and the contemporary world so insightfully that they speak of it and apply it with a creativity that helps unpack its obvious relevance. The Bible is the Spirit's book, and in healthy churches you sense that the Spirit is speaking, convicting and guiding through Scripture.

7. **There is openness to the Spirit.** No, this does not have to mean charismatic mania – ecstatic experiences – but it does mean that there is a tangible awareness that we don't own the church. Nor do we guide the church. We are a community of the Spirit. We should never be so precious about our planned and structured programmes that we quench the Spirit.

8. **It is prophetic.** By this I mean courageous enough to name, address and engage the issues of the day – and the days to come. This is not church as a comfortable ghetto of irrelevance, but church as actively and sacrificially incarnated in the midst of struggle. It is about being church in such a way that we all become bigger, and find the courage to embark upon healthy journeys we would otherwise have been too timid to take.

9. **It is a place of change.** Nothing is more exhilarating than being in a church where you sense that all are on a journey of wholesome change. Pettiness recedes when people genuinely opt for needed change, because change is hard, and when we embark upon it we quickly realize we will only make it if we are there for one another, encouraging each other each step of the way. Change comes in many forms. For some it will be trying out a new skill; for others, a personal growth programme; for yet others, losing weight or stopping smoking or taking a spiritual retreat or risking a new career that will serve and help others or engaging in political protest or . . . you get the idea.

10. **It is diverse.** Healthy churches are not homogeneous. They don't duplicate the local tennis club. They are not filled with people just like us. They bring diverse people together as a foretaste of the promise in the Bible that people from every race and tribe will enter into the future that God has ultimately planned for this planet.

11. **It makes a difference.** Healthy churches make a difference to their community. The community would miss them if they closed their doors. While members of the church care for each other, there is a healthy outward focus in the church. The concern extends both to and beyond their immediate community. You sense

that the people are global citizens and often work cooperatively with other groups to make a difference in countries other than their own. Healthy churches often surprise you by the extent of their impact as the combined effort of their members is greater than if they had each been working on their own.

12. **It is not all about the leader.** While healthy churches are well led by gifted and called people of integrity and character, they are not all about the leader. Participation levels are high. Church is not a spectator sport. In its healthy version it engages and involves. While there are times when some may need time out to sit quietly on the sideline to recover from a life that has become too busy or been too painful, even from the sideline there is a gentle flow of support and encouragement both to and from whoever happens to be on the frontline at the time.

Do such churches exist? Absolutely! There is likely to be one not far from where you live. And if you get involved in it, you may well conclude that Christianity is probably true.

If you are a reader who believes that Christianity is probably untrue, you may have read the section above with some bemusement. You may even feel that the need to include guidelines on how to spot a healthy church indicates a deep underlying problem, and that the implication is that most expressions of Christianity are toxic and best avoided. However, Jesus himself warned that false versions of Christianity would abound. Ironically, if there weren't counterfeit versions of Christianity, it would mean that Jesus was mistaken when he predicted them (see, for example, Matthew 24:5,11), and that would count against belief in him.

We have earlier looked at some of the damaging things the church has done in its history. Almost without exception, these have been times when Christians have disobeyed the teaching of Jesus. When the church embarked on the Crusades, a terrible and indefensible time in the history of the faith, it was in direct disobedience to Jesus' teaching that those who live by the sword will die by the sword (Matthew 26:52) and that his kingdom was not of this world (John 18:36).

Put differently, it is when Christianity has failed to act in accordance with its own teaching that it has done harm. While we should not be inherently suspicious of everything that goes in the name of Christianity, when evaluating any expression of faith it is sensible to ask if it is a logical extension of the teaching of Jesus. If not, we should be wary of evaluating Christianity in the light of the particular example we are exploring.

In our next chapter, we will weigh up where this evidence and these pointers leads us . . .

7

Let's Weigh This Up

In weighing up the evidence of the last two chapters, let's remember the basic task of this book. We have set out to explore the three chief accusations against Christianity, namely that it is intellectually vacuous, morally suspect and experientially empty. In the last two chapters we have explored the claim that it is morally suspect.

There are undoubtedly instances when the Christian faith has fallen well short of its own ideals. We have noted that at times the church has failed to adequately protect children, and some have been physically and sexually abused as a result. No one would want to minimize the seriousness of such a failure or ignore the tragic long-term consequences suffered by the victims of this evil.

There are times in the history of the church when it has held significant power and has used that power to further the ends of a handful of entitled clergy. In some of its worst moments the church has tried to coerce belief (or at least conformity) at the point of the sword or on threat of imprisonment. I belong to the tribe of Christians known as Baptist, and some of my forebears were persecuted as a result of their conviction that baptism should take place after conversion to Christianity and that it should be by full immersion in water. Some of the early Baptists were drowned with the cynical catchcry, 'If they want water, they shall have it.' This should never have happened, and no serious attempt can be made to defend those who acted so heartlessly.

We have celebrated the scientific breakthroughs that occurred as a result of the Christian faith of those who made them. While there is a tendency in the twenty-first century to view their faith as incidental to their work, these scientists would have had none of this, as even a cursory glance at their writings reveals, for they spoke repeatedly of the majesty and glory of God and the way in which their faith inspired their quest. Yet for all that, many scientists were treated most shabbily by the church, often simply for discovering a truth that the church had not anticipated and which it initially reacted poorly to.

While we rightly lament each of these significant failures, let's not forget what the failure was. It was a failure not of the Christian faith, but of the Christian church to act in a Christian manner. This is an extremely important point. Every failure of Christianity has been its failure to be Christian. It is not the faith that is defective. It is our inadequate obedience to it. What is needed therefore is not a rejection of the Christian faith, but a firm refusal to accept counterfeit or substandard versions of faith.

Of course there is a risk in this. When does a refusal to accept a substandard version of faith turn into a heresy trial, or a vicious onslaught on someone who sees things in a different light? We must not be naive about the potential risks in advocating pure forms of the Christian faith.

The safeguard is eminently simple. Responses to alternative views of faith must be Christian. We earlier noted Paul's comment in Ephesians 2:20 that the church should be built on the teaching of the apostles and prophets, with Christ Jesus as the cornerstone. So let's do this. If we are tempted to abuse someone for holding a different version of faith from our own, let's recall the words of Jesus: 'Those who live by the sword will die by the sword.' Jesus said them because he meant us to take them seriously, and to exclude violence from the list of options at our disposal. The church has erred each time it has forgotten that. In other words, it has erred when it has forgotten what it means to follow the teaching of Jesus.

It is grossly unfair to cite only the failures of the church in history. A much more objective way to assess the impact of the Christian faith on history is to also note some of its most significant achievements (respect for the sanctity of life and the value of all people; the abolition of slavery; rights for women, children and workers; education for all; health care for all; multiple scientific breakthroughs – and that's hardly a complete list), and to consider its impact on those societies which have most fully embraced its teaching.

The latter is a significant test. Take a map of the world. Note those countries which were most impacted by Christianity, and especially by the Protestant Reformation. By and large these are countries that have prospered. They are certainly not perfect, but the protections they offer minorities are significant, and they demand high levels of accountability from their elected officials. The very significant majority take democracy extremely seriously and are usually willing to self-critique their own role in the world. Almost all of these countries are considered desirable destinations for the tens of millions of refugees and asylum seekers in the world today.

This simple observation makes a mockery of those who attempt to suggest that the impact of Christianity on human history has been toxic. The common sense of ordinary people makes its own very powerful statement. This faith works. It might not have always got everything right in history, but it got it significantly better than any other ideology.

Today we are encouraged by many of the New Atheists to embrace secularism as a pathway to human freedom and happiness. It is difficult to know why anyone would embark upon such a hazardous, indeed reckless, path, given the shocking failure of the secular states of the twentieth century.

While Christianity is able to point to one country after another which flourished as a result of embracing the Christian faith, the harvest of secularism is uniformly bleak. True, most of its expressions were in the various communist experiments of the last century, but do not be quick to excuse these, or to pretend that the atrocities committed were unrelated to the abandonment of faith. Believing there to be no God to account to, the leaders of these regimes descended to what were probably the lowest levels in all of human history. The resulting death toll is disputed: the most optimistic suggestion is that 21 million people lost their lives as a result; more sobering calculations suggest a figure closer to 100 million.[1]

The New Atheists quickly take offence when such figures are quoted, assuring us that their version of the secular state would be dramatically different. Even more perversely, they sometimes try to blame faith for the atrocities in atheistic communist states, suggesting, for example, that the prior embrace of faith in Communist Russia led to unquestioning acceptance of authority, making possible the atrocities under Stalin. (Hmm, really? Talk about not allowing anything to count against your hypothesis!) Such glibness strikes me as deeply irresponsible. If we will not learn from history, we are likely to repeat it.

In weighing the moral contribution of Christianity, there are so many enormously positive achievements to point to. The key reason these achievements are mentioned relatively rarely is because of Christianity itself. It encourages its followers to be humble, and a little introspective, asking not what can be praised from the past but what can be done better. At times this tendency is our undoing. But let's not be naive – the life of Jesus has changed the fortunes of this planet for good in a way that no other life has. Why, we even date the current year as a close approximation to the number of years from his birth. For let's be clear about it. The birth of Jesus changed almost everything. In fact, his life has been enough to convince around 2 billion people that Christianity is probably true.

Section C

But Faith is Experientially Empty

8

So Here's the Problem: Faith is Experientially Empty

I went to a high school where the custom was to begin each school day by singing a dreary hymn and then reciting the Lord's Prayer. We had to keep a copy of the small hymn book in our back pocket and were required to produce it at periodic hymn-book checks. If we didn't have it on us, we were caned. Saying the Lord's Prayer was a hurried affair, those in my small circle having a competition to see who could get through it first; under eight seconds was considered impressive.

Perhaps that's your impression of religion: a dull ritual interrupting the flow of an otherwise happy life. It's the third of the accusations of the New Atheists – that faith is not only intellectually vacuous and morally suspect but also experientially empty. As their bus adverts proclaim: 'There's probably no God. Now stop worrying and enjoy your life.'

The charge is usually made at one of two levels.

Superficially, it is that faith practices such as church attendance and the like are insufferably dull. Belief in God seems to spoil our fun, not only through tedious rituals but also by making us feel guilty and anxious about our ordinary human foibles.

But there is another level at which the issue is addressed – that of deep disappointment with God, or profound hurt that God (or the God who doesn't exist) should allow a world with such deep pain. It might be accompanied by outrage: 'You say that God is love. Then why . . . ?', and a genuinely painful, sometimes hauntingly tragic, tale is told.

I remember a church picnic held after a morning service at the first church where I served as pastor, in South Africa. We were in a beautiful park close to the church, with the stunning Jonkershoek Mountains as our backdrop.

One of our regular attenders had brought her husband along. It was unusual for him to be there, so I tried to get to know him. He was an older man, and surprisingly aggressive in his attitude towards me. After my attempt at a few pleasantries he suddenly burst out, 'Don't think that because I have attended your picnic that I for one minute agree with or condone what you are doing. I'm here because my wife wanted to come – and she matters to me. I was taught to believe in God as a child, and I did. Then the war came along. I, and many in my squadron, were captured and taken as prisoners of war. I saw things I never believed possible. Unspeakable cruelty – such suffering. And I prayed that God would end it. But the only answer I received was silence . . . nothing, nothing at all. I was the only one from my squadron who survived. They didn't die quietly. Such mindless, senseless, brutal suffering – and then the silence of death. It matched the silence of God. Nothing there – nothing at all. Don't talk to me about the God of love. And don't even think of replying with some senseless platitude.'

I heeded his instruction and said nothing. He was close to tears and walked away from me rapidly. The war had ended over forty years before that conversation took place, but for that man the pain of what had taken place was as current as if it was yesterday. How do you get over some of life's most traumatic events, and can you believe in a God of love if you have experienced unspeakable cruelty?

We have already noted the adage that the 'proof of the pudding is in the eating'. Our life experience will inevitably shape what we are able or unable to believe.

Undoubtedly many have found the Christian faith to be the source of great joy, support, encouragement and inspiration. It has sparked their finest efforts and been responsible for their noblest endeavours. But others simply lament an absent God, or a God who never comes through for them or for those they care about.

How are we to make sense of this?

One of the oldest theological questions is that of **theodicy**; that is, if God is all-loving, all-knowing, present everywhere and all-powerful, why does suffering exist? It is the combination of these attributes that makes atheists declare belief in the Christian God to be unsustainable.

Think it through.

When confronted by suffering we could conclude, 'God does not care'; but the Christian faith will not allow this, for it proclaims a God of love. We could say, 'God is loving, but unfortunately didn't know about this situation and therefore didn't act'; but again the Christian faith rejects this hypothesis, as it declares that God is all-knowing and speaks of God's omniscience. We could also suggest that God would have acted, but didn't happen to be in the vicinity; but that doesn't work because we declare God to be omnipresent. Another solution could be that God, while loving, knowing and present, sadly lacks the power to do anything about it. Of course such a response would meet with an equally quick rejection by all Christians, who put their faith in an all-powerful God, or a God who is omnipotent.

When you put these claims together – God is all-loving, God is all-knowing, God is present everywhere and God is all-powerful – you start to realize that the theodicy question seriously challenges these claims, and you are able to understand why some people who have suffered greatly find it impossible to believe in God.

In the next chapter we will look at some of the ways Christians have resolved this dilemma – at least to their own satisfaction.

Those who find belief in God impossible often cite another factor when it comes to the realm of experience. They note that those who believe in God seem to have erratic God experiences. In other words, while they sometimes feel close to God, at other times God seems to be far removed from them. Even some of the spiritual greats struggled with this. St John of the Cross wrote about the 'dark night of the soul', those times when God seems to be absent and when, no matter how much one longs for God's presence, no breakthrough occurs. St John of the Cross was not the only one to note the experience, Mother Teresa also speaking of passing through a similar wilderness.

This objection is probably best summarized as follows: 'If Christians claim that God wants to be in communication with humans, why does God make it so difficult, so that even the saintliest sometimes struggle to feel close to God? Surely if God is real, it would be a little easier!'

Atheists often claim that Christians hold on to an imaginary friend, God, and are themselves puzzled that the presence of the imaginary friend occasionally seems more real than at other times, but usually conclude that our power of self-delusion is more effective at some periods than at others. They suggest that the 'dark night of the soul' is just a moment of confronting the truth that one's belief is mythical, a time when the believer is forced to come face to face with the ultimate aloneness which all human beings must endure. It is not uncommon for them to identify with the experience, for many atheists are people who once believed but now find belief impossible.

The question of why some Christians lose their faith is related to this. Sometimes they are people who once claimed a close relationship with God, and might even have spoken about times when they were very conscious of the presence of God. Some even pointed others to faith and persuaded them to believe in the God they now find themselves rejecting.

How do we explain experiences like this?

Those who don't believe often frame the loss of faith around an account of growing maturity, a willingness to accept life as it is, of no longer needing a God hypothesis to help them make it through the day. Whereas once they needed an imaginary friend, they no longer do. They would say that religion was a helpful crutch for a while, but in the end they came to the conclusion that they needed it no longer, and that in reality it was holding them back, stopping them from facing truth, and preventing them from becoming all they could be.

Is religious faith a sign of emotional immaturity – a security blanket that some need to hold on to? It is certainly an accusation that is frequently made by those who don't believe, and must be considered as we ask whether or not Christianity is probably true.

There are of course Christians who claim they have had dramatic experiences of the presence of God. Sometimes they declare that God has miraculously intervened in their lives and done what they thought would be impossible. It is not uncommon to hear a claim of healing from a very serious ailment, and that often after a period of serious prayer.

For those who believe, such encounters are often a decisive proof of the existence of God.

Atheists are, however, more sceptical, and accuse Christians of having a poor grasp of statistics. While they do not deny that some Christians have been cured from forms of cancer that have a survival rate of only one in a hundred, or even one in a thousand, they quickly counter that of course that happens – in about one in a hundred cases, or one in a thousand cases. What Christians proclaim as miraculous, they consider to be little more than the inevitability of long odds coming off from time to time, and in much the ratio that should be expected.

So what are we to make of this? Is faith something you grow out of after a while? Is it experientially empty, and are those who hold on to it likely to experience a major let-down in the foreseeable future? We will explore this in the next chapter.

9

But Have You Considered? The Witness of Faith from the Inside

The chorus of a popular but now dated Christian song puts the question, 'You ask me how I know he lives?' and answers, 'He lives within my heart.'[1] It is the answer vast numbers of Christians would give if asked why they believe that God is real and can be known through Jesus Christ. In essence, they would point to their experience. They would tell you that prayer is a meaningful spiritual discipline, and that through it, they have often experienced the presence of God. They would describe lofty times of worship when it felt that God was closer to them than the person they were standing next to. Many would have dramatic stories to tell of how God answered a prayer in a time of crisis, or of how a Bible passage spoke to them and provided direction for a perplexing and worrying problem. When you boil it down, they are saying, 'You ask me how I know he lives? He lives within my heart.' Their answer is genuine, and while it may not convince you, it convinces them; after all, it is their experience, not yours, and they know if they are telling the truth or not. It is reasonable to assume that the majority continue in the Christian faith because their experience convinces them of its veracity.

Francis Spufford is right when he notes: 'it is still a mistake to suppose that it is assent to the propositions that makes you a believer. It is the feelings that are primary. I assent to the ideas because I have the feelings; I don't have the feelings because I've assented to the ideas.'[2]

While many are dismissive of the evidence of personal experience, it is foolish to ignore the witness of those who are insiders of the faith. By and large, their claims are what would be expected if God is real and does communicate with humans. The fact that hundreds of millions of people both today, and throughout the pages of history, have claimed such experiences must be given some weight. To cite the quote often repeated by the New Atheists, 'Absence of evidence is evidence of absence.' But this is not an absence of evidence. To the contrary, it is an embarrassment of evidence, the witness of hundreds of millions of people throughout the centuries. It cannot be lightly ignored.

Not that it is always plain sailing for those who believe in God. They too are impacted by the struggles and pain of life, and there is no evidence to suggest that being a Christian immunizes you against misfortune.

I have been a pastor for over thirty years, and in that time I have heard people express confusion again and again about the way God works. While they haven't always said 'God's not fair' or that they are disappointed with God, it's clear that's how they feel.

Sometimes it is more dramatic than disappointment. It is rage and anger. I once had a man explode at me after witnessing some terrible atrocities. 'I no longer believe in God,' he said. 'But if there is a God, then frankly I don't think much of him!'

At other times it is not anger but more a sense of despair. I remember listening to a man for whom nothing ever seemed to go right expressing his pain with an endless series of 'why's. He was struggling with depression and saw no way beyond an endless period of black heaviness that settled each day and usually lasted for hours and hours. 'Why does nothing ever go right for me? I've really tried to serve God. You tell me what I've done wrong? And yet nothing ever comes together? Why does God allow it?'

Then there are the questions that, while unspoken, hang heavily in the air. I have sat with a young family who were trying to come to terms with the death of their 5-year-old from leukaemia. They were too stunned and numbed to articulate any questions, but in my heart I was asking them. 'God, I knew that little boy . . . why did you allow this?'

Often it's not so dramatic but is still perplexing. I remember a congregant who had purchased a new car complaining that someone had run a key from one end to the other along the sparkling new paintwork. 'I've never had a new car before,' she said. 'I was so excited with it. Why did it have to happen with the new car? It wouldn't have mattered with the old one. Isn't God supposed to look after things like that? After all, I'm doing my best to serve him.'

So, what are we to make of those experiences that don't make sense? How are we to live with the questions we are not even prepared to put into words for fear of where the sentiment might lead us? Situations like this raise questions for everyone. How are we to explain the pain and injustice of life?

Atheists have a relatively easy explanation, albeit one that fails to inspire and in no way lightens the load. (But if you are an atheist you feel no need to inspire or to lighten the load, so probably don't view that as a problem.) I can hear an atheist friend of mine saying it: 'There is nothing to explain. It is just the way it is. There is no essential purpose behind the universe. If there is no purpose, nothing requires explanation. It is simply the way that it is. Ultimately put your life experience down to luck. Some strike it lucky; some not. But, hey, even if you don't, no need to stress too much. In the end, we're all dead. Those for whom life rolled a double six will be just as dead as you in twenty, forty or a hundred years. For everyone, this is the end. So, enjoy life if you can and for as long as you can.'

This view offers nothing other than a claim that an explanation is unnecessary and, indeed, impossible. It flies in the face of the deep intuition of the vast majority of people that life does have a basic meaning and purpose and that their life counts for something.

Most of us feel connected to a larger story, and when misfortune prevents us from pursuing that narrative we find it impossible to ask anything other than 'Why?' And that very question – why? – says it all. We instinctively assume purpose, and rebel against life experiences that frustrate that sense of purpose. Without wishing to sound too clever, we must ask why the 'why'? Why, at a deeply experiential level, do we default to an assumption of purpose? Could this point to a deeper truth – that instinctively we grasp that we are created beings, and that if we are created, there is a creator?

But if there is purpose behind the universe, and if that purpose has been given by a loving, just and generous God, why do many people suffer? Does the Christian story have sufficient explanatory power to cope with the problem of evil and suffering?

Let's be clear. The Christian account of reality has at its heart an explanation for the pain and the brokenness of the world. It suggests that rather than shake our fist at God because of suffering, we should take a deep inward look and recognize that our rebellion against God, and our unwillingness to follow the guidance and leading of the one who created us, led to the fall of humanity. Because of our sinfulness, the world is not as it should be, and all of creation groans and misfires as a result. The world has become a pale shadow of what it was meant to be. The good news is that God has provided a pathway to forgiveness and restoration through the death of Jesus on the cross. Those who wish to avail themselves of this forgiveness can have a new start in their relationship with God. That relationship provides them with a key to eternity, and it is in eternity that all things are rectified.

True, that is perhaps too short and simplistic a summary of the Christian faith, but it provides an adequate start. Ask why there is suffering in the world, and the Christian faith points to the fall of humanity, while providing the hope that in the future all wrongs will be set to right. We can therefore say that Christianity views justice as an eschatological category – in other words, ultimate justice only comes in the course of eternity – and eternity lasts well beyond any single lifetime on this planet. While justice will reign, it is an eventual, not an immediate, reign. And when it does reign, all wrongs will be put right.

This may sound a little too theoretical for some, especially for those whose life experience has included great suffering or who have observed the pain of others.

In the previous chapter we stated the key components of the theodicy question. Let's do so again . . .

Christians believe in a God who is all-loving, all-powerful, all-knowing and always present. If God didn't love, or wasn't all-powerful, or didn't know, or couldn't get to us, perhaps we could find an excuse for the lack of divine intervention in the atrocities of life. But we do not believe in a God with limited ability, and so the question 'Is God unfair?' can't be avoided.

Though I've given a broad overview of the question and some possible answers, let's try to unpack the options a little more systematically. We will do this by looking at the suffering of Job.

The Bible tells the story of a man named Job who was so good that God boasted to Satan about Job's many virtues. Satan replied that Job only worshipped God because God showed him so much kindness, and suggested this would quickly evaporate if Job faced any serious suffering. As a test of Job's genuineness, God allows Satan to tempt and test Job with many horrible trials, so much so that Job is often seen to symbolize those whose suffer greatly and unfairly.

As Job asks the question 'Why am I suffering?', let's explore some possible answers that can be given.[3]

Possibility 1: God doesn't exist – get over it!

Strangely, the answer an atheist would give to Job is probably the most unsatisfying in times of trial. It is as though we instinctively realize that there has to be someone to blame or to hold to account for what is taking place. More fundamentally, if there is no God to reach out to, our situation is truly without hope. Prayer seems to be hard-wired into our human make-up. Even those who very rarely pray can find themselves praying in times of serious trouble, often to their own confusion ('Why am I praying? I don't even believe in God!'). More than a fair few people have come to faith as a direct result of a serious crisis they went through. Often their witness is that despite being unsure if there was a God to help them and, if there was, whether they were entitled to ask for help, they did ask, and God came through for them. For them, crisis was the pathway to faith.

Similarly, I have noticed that the faith of many people has become stronger as a result of a crisis, not because they found an easy answer (many did not and simply have to live with a new and difficult reality) but because they claim to have sensed the presence of God more closely during their crisis, even though God seemed to be doing nothing tangible to solve it.

While it seems deeply counter-intuitive, I have come to the conclusion that pain is more likely than pleasure to lead to a close experience of God. And those who have been through such experiences are often the most adamant that God is real. While you would think their experience would open them to atheism, ironically atheism is least appealing at such times.

Are there exceptions to this? Of course! But what is generally true is generally true, and this is an interesting general truth. Most people instinctively reject the answer 'God doesn't exist – get over it!' Furthermore, they are usually the most rejecting of this answer during times of suffering.

Possibility 2: God is unfair – get used to it!

Though we may be uncomfortable saying it, perhaps God is unfair. True, it's a statement we don't like, and something inside us usually rebels at the thought of making it. Accepting it highlights our impotence in the face of God. It is rather like saying, 'Unfortunately it turns out that God is awful and there is nothing we can do about it.' It is a position seriously at odds with what Christians have traditionally believed and taught about God.

As an onlooker of Job's suffering, Job's wife reaches the conclusion that God is unfair – case closed. She gives the advice, 'Are you still maintaining your integrity? Curse God and die!' (Job 2:9). Her position is clear. Give up on God. Be bold enough to shake your fist at God, say 'Life stinks' and depart. There is nothing we can do about the injustice that comes the way of some people, but we can at least be honest enough to voice our disgust.

Remember that this was advice spoken by a fellow sufferer. While Job's wife didn't have the illness that attacked him, she had also lost her children and wealth (Job 1). Sometimes if you love someone, you suffer almost as much as they do when you see them struggling. When you watch it from the perspective of your own broken heart . . . well, don't be too quick to judge Job's wife. Hers was not an easy lot.

Job's wife was furious with God and adamant that God is unfair. What is more, she was prepared to tell God so. With time she changed her position. Her difficult situation passed, and the family fortunes were restored. Sometimes we resign ourselves to what seems to be God's lack of fairness and then alter our perspective further down the line. In many instances shaking our fist at an unfair God turns out to be a premature response.

Possibility 3: God is not unfair – it's all our fault

This was the option Job's friends opted for. As you go through the remarkable story of Job's suffering you find that Job's friends encourage him to believe his anguish is a result of his sin. It is easy to follow their logic. God is always good and kind, so if someone is suffering, it stands to reason that it's their own fault. Job was struggling, so obviously he had some fault they were not aware of. One of the friends, Zophar, assures Job that if he will only devote himself to God and put his sin away, all will be well for him again (Job 11:13–20).

Many Christians have fallen prey to the logic of Job's suspect friends. Some preachers have promised people health, wealth and prosperity if they will only trust God fully, and have then blamed the struggler's lack of faith if they achieved anything less than excellent health and material wealth.

Now it is true that God's grace is such that we often receive generous gifts. But when the good gifts don't come there is no reason to conclude that it is because of our sin. It could be, but most of the Bible's heroes suffered. Usually it had nothing to do with sin. The apostle Paul, who did more than anyone to advance the spread of Christianity, suffered from a mysterious ailment which he labelled a 'thorn in the flesh' (see 2 Corinthians 12:7). What had Paul done to deserve this?

Job's suffering was because he was so good that God agreed he could be tested. The Bible tells us that the prophet Jeremiah had a dreadful life, filled with repeated humiliations and great suffering. We remember him as the wailing prophet, but he was faithful to God. And think about the story of Hosea, whose wife turns to prostitution.

Part of the reason why Job's story is recorded in Scripture is to remind us that the trite and hurtful logic of Job's friends just doesn't work when life is unfair. Drawing a straight line between sin and suffering is untrue in most cases. Among other things, it forgets that we are both 'sinners and sinned against', and that much of our suffering results because we have been 'sinned against'.

That is not to suggest that the Bible doesn't see the origin of suffering as lying in the rebellion of humanity against God as recorded in Genesis 2 and 3, but it does remind us that there is no necessary link between the suffering of a particular individual and their sin.

Possibility 4: God is nice but not as powerful as we think

When we say that God is unfair, we may be working on a false assumption. Rabbi Harold Kushner in a popular book, *When Bad Things Happen to Good People*, takes an unusual line.[4] Having watched his son die of progeria, Kushner had suffered at a deeply personal level. His response was not to blame God but rather to say that God also thinks that life is unfair. Unfortunately God is not powerful enough to be able to do anything about it. Kushner proposes a perfectly pleasant and kindly God, but one who lacks power. God is as frustrated, even outraged, by the condition of the world as we are, but is just as stumped as to what to do about it.

However, you have to ask who Kushner is talking about. Is the God of the Bible really incapable of acting? Whose help did God need when making the world? There are so many stories in the Bible that record God's intervention in impossibly difficult circumstances, and each affirms that God has the power to work everything out for good. Whatever portrait of God Kushner is trying to paint, it is not a picture of the God of the Bible.

Possibility 5: Unfairness all turns out for the best

This is an option we often adopt. Sometimes it is true. We're urged to turn 'scars into stars'! If we're suffering, it's surely that we're being tested and strengthened, and the resilience we develop during such periods is beneficial. Now it is good to be positive when difficult things happen to us, but to try and pretend that we have answered the question 'Is God unfair?' simply by suggesting that suffering toughens us . . . well, that's trite!

A friend of mine, a brilliant mathematician now sidelined for several decades by chronic fatigue syndrome, wryly commented, 'I'm sure that I've learnt a lot through this, and have become very deep and profound, but I don't see what the point of being so wise is if I'm never well enough to mix with others and pass on my insights!'

And who benefits when innocent children suffer? If I'm supposed to be made into a better and more profound person because of the suffering of others, surely it is not fair to them. Clearly we can't settle for this answer alone.

Possibility 6: We are looking at this the wrong way

If none of the five answers we've given so far is really adequate, perhaps we need to look at the question in a different way.

Philip Yancey in his book *Disappointment with God* tells of asking a man he knew had suffered greatly if he was disappointed with God.[5] To his surprise Duncan, whose life had been radically altered by a car accident and who also had to cope with his wife's advancing cancer, replied quite firmly that he wasn't disappointed with God at all.

'But surely, after all that has happened to you?' Yancey queried.

'No,' the man replied. 'You're confusing God with life. God isn't life. He's God! Life's not fair, but God is good!'

Now that's worth thinking about!

Life isn't fair. The Bible is clear about why it isn't. The world has been tainted by the fall. Things no longer work properly. After their sin, Adam and Eve were warned that from then on, the earth would only produce food because of the sweat of their brow. Childbirth would bring pain. Relationships between men and women would be strained (Genesis 3:16–19). Because of sin, life is no longer fair. The world is not as it was made to be.

So does that mean that God is the kindly but impotent figure portrayed by Rabbi Kushner, wishing things were better but incapable of doing anything about it?

No! The God of the Bible is the God who is deeply dissatisfied with the unfairness of the world – so dissatisfied that God's judgement sits upon this present age. God has promised to make a new heaven and a new earth. The present one is simply not good enough.

'Oh, fine,' you say. 'Pie in the sky in the sweet by and by!'

It is more radical than that. Life's not fair, but God does not leave us to face it on our own. That's the message of God becoming one of us – the message of Jesus' incarnation in Bethlehem's stable and of his life among us. It is the promise of the crucified-but-now-risen Jesus: 'I am with you always, to the very end of the age' (Matthew 28:20).

Because of the fall we live in an unfair world. Poet William Blake (1757–1827) writes in 'Auguries of Innocence':

Every morn and every night,
some are born to sweet delight.
Some are born to sweet delight,
some are born to endless night.

Regardless of whether their lot is sweet delight or endless night, Christians claim to worship a crucified and risen God who has suffered and struggled and become one of us. They claim that this God does not desert us in our hour of need. They argue that God is the first to acknowledge that the perfect has not yet come, but that God promises that it will, and that God is with us wherever our life journey might lead.

Furthermore, because God is love, even though Christians are aware that they will never turn this world into a utopia, they are convinced that God calls us to follow a path of love so that this world might become a gentler, kinder place, even while they wait for the promise of the future. The Christian church is formed for many purposes, but one is to be a community of care – a sign of God's love for the world. Life might not be fair, but it is certainly a lot easier when lived with people who love, care for and support you.

In summary, then, the Christian response to suffering is that life's not fair, but God is good. And God is with us. And we can be there for one another. And in the end, God will have the new heaven and the new earth ready for us.

There is little doubt that this is a more hopeful narrative than the atheist's shrug of the shoulder, and dismissive 'That's the way it is – get over it'. But is it true, or simply wishful thinking? Clearly this is the crunch question. Are we simply whistling in the dark, desperately hoping for an explanation when in fact there is none? Or is there some basis to suggest that this might well be an accurate portrayal of reality?

In this chapter we are looking at the evidence of personal experience. Earlier in the book (chapter 3) we looked at some of the intellectual arguments for belief. We noted in chapter 6 that these arguments have been backed up by a track record in history that, while blemished at points, is most impressive – indeed, with no near competitor. The overall thrust of our argument is simple: no one single point will settle the case decisively; it is the accumulation of evidence that matters.

Put differently, the fact that there are significant intellectual reasons to believe in the truthfulness of the Christian message (chapter 3), backed up by Christianity's track record of having changed the world for the good (chapter 6), further supplemented by literally millions of accounts of individuals speaking about the experiential reality of the Christian faith (chapter 9) . . . well, it makes a pretty convincing case, one built up by strong pieces of evidence gleaned from different realms.

You might ask, 'But how can you say that millions of people claim some significant encounter with God?'

Because it's true!

A 2006 Pew Forum report on Christians from ten countries – most in the developing world – found that around 200 million Christians in the charismatic tradition (let me repeat that: 200 million) claimed that they had personally experienced or witnessed divine healing. Lest you say, 'That's charismatic Christians for you. They're always looking for miracles', the same study found that a third of Christians from these countries who are not from a charismatic or Pentecostal tradition also reported having witnessed or experienced divine healing.

Now while some of these claims may be false, to suggest that all 200 million of them are false is a bold claim. As I said earlier, this is not an absence of evidence; it is an embarrassment of evidence.

And there is more evidence besides. One of the countries not included in the study was China, where the Christian church has been growing strongly for decades. The China Christian Council says that approximately half of the conversion growth in the country can be attributed to experiences of faith healing. In other words, 50% of those new to the Christian faith in China (and there are many millions of them) have come to faith as a direct result of what they consider to be a miracle.

These results, plus the many accounts of miracles found in the New Testament, are discussed far more fully (as in 1,172 pages more fully) in Craig S. Keener's outstanding two-volume work *Miracles: The Credibility of the New Testament Accounts*.[6] It is a book that deeply challenges our assumption that miracles rarely (if ever) happen.

You may remember from our earlier discussion of miracles (chapter 3) that the eighteenth-century Scottish philosopher David Hume argued that miracles do not happen based on the assumed widespread absence of occurrence of miracles. That is, miracles don't happen, so they can't happen. His argument has often been used in a circular way: miracles don't happen, therefore the claim that a miracle happened can't be true, because miracles don't happen. But Keener's extraordinarily well-documented book provides evidence of miracles from Asia, Africa, Latin America and the Caribbean. The problem with Hume was that his eighteenth-century Scottish world was so tiny. He simply didn't have access to the vast array of material now available. And to say it yet one more time, no one can now suggest that there is an absence of evidence for the miraculous. There is only an embarrassment of evidence. When you have over 200 million witnesses, the need for explanation shifts from those who believe to those who do not believe. How many more million witnesses are necessary? Or is the question being approached with a closed mind by those who stubbornly hold on to disbelief?

This may still sound a little too theoretical for some readers, who might be thinking, 'It's lovely for those who have had an experience like that, but I can't say it has happened for me.'

Let me, therefore, explore how the realm of experience works out for many Christians. In fact, rather than generalize, let me tell you how it has worked out for me. Now I realize that you might dismiss what I am about to write, asking, 'Why would I believe you?' Obviously, I can't make you believe me, but perhaps you will hear the heartbeat behind what I am writing. Like most people, I have needed reasons for both head and heart to be able to place my trust and confidence in Jesus and to build my life on his teaching. And I have found them. I would imagine my having been a Christian pastor for well over thirty years would convince you that I have stuck to my calling for this long because I have at least convinced myself that what I hold to is true.

So how does the experience of faith work out for me on an everyday basis?

I can only say that I sense that I am accompanied on my life journey. True, some will find that difficult to accept, and might suggest that I am deluding myself with imaginary friends. But that is not how I experience my life – and I can only experience it as I experience it. There are reasons why I feel accompanied. Let me give a few examples.

In 2002 I was invited to apply for the position I currently hold as Principal of Vose Seminary, in Perth, Australia. I and my family were living in Auckland, New Zealand at the time, where I was happily serving as the senior pastor of Mt Roskill Baptist Church. Actually, I was so content in my ministry at Mt Roskill that the invitation to apply for this post was most unsettling. As Vose Seminary had an outstanding history of training people to be pastors and leaders in the Christian church, it was flattering to be considered for the role, and I also knew that such a position would be both strategic and satisfying. But my wife, Rosemary, and I were happy at Mt Roskill, and our three children were less than enthusiastic at the thought of possibly moving to another country. Half-heartedly, I let my name be considered for the post, and sent the requested CV and answered a set of candidate questions, which was followed by many more questions.

Then there was silence – for weeks and weeks. 'Ah well,' I thought, 'so much for that. We got ourselves worked up and flustered for nothing.'

To my surprise, however, just as I thought nothing was happening, I was asked to answer another set of questions. I looked at the length of the questions asked, and reflected that the process had now been going on for many months, the family had been unsettled for long enough, and, given that I was still being questioned, I was presumably not the right person for the job. I decided to pull out of the process, and happily settled back into my life as senior pastor at Mt Roskill, while doing some part-time lecturing for two of the local theological colleges in Auckland.

Months went by. Then one night – I don't know why and I don't know how – I suddenly had a compelling sense that I needed to phone the Baptist Churches of Western Australia, who own Vose Seminary and oversee it as part of their wider ministry, and to ask them about the principal's post. I wasn't really sure what I was supposed to ask, but inwardly had a strong sense that I was meant to be the next principal of Vose Seminary, that I should never have withdrawn my application, and that if I didn't do something then and there, it would be beyond reversing. It was 10.30 p.m. in Auckland so 6.30 p.m. in Perth.

'Too late,' I thought. 'Their offices close at 5 p.m.; there will be no one there.'

But all I can say is that as I decided to delay phoning until the next day, an inner voice said very strongly, 'Phone now. You must phone now.'

I still clearly remember walking out of the kitchen and down the stairs into my study to make the call. I phoned, expecting no reply.

The phone was answered within a few rings. Steve Smith, the then Director of Ministries for the Baptist Churches of Western Australia, was on the line. As I heard his voice I realized I didn't have any idea of what I was supposed to say to him, so I mumbled a little and said something like, 'Hi Steve. Don't know if you remember me from our discussions about the principal's post at Vose. It's been a while now, and I'm just interested to know who you appointed.'

Steve said, 'Interesting that you've phoned now. We haven't made the appointment yet, but I'm just about to go into a meeting that will finalize our shortlist of candidates for interview. I always felt you were the right person for Vose. Tell me you are willing to reinstate your application and I'll make sure you are shortlisted. Just as well you phoned when you did. Tomorrow would have been too late.'

The rest is history. I got the post, and it has been absolutely the right one for both me, my family and Vose Seminary.

What do you make of my claim of a strong sense – almost of compulsion – that I had to phone that night? You might dismiss the account saying, 'Frankly, I don't believe you. I know preachers and their stories. They always exaggerate and make something out of nothing', and think nothing more of it. After all, it happened to me, not to you, so why should you spend much time thinking about it?

That would be a fair point, but to state the obvious, I am me! And it happened to me. I can't just ignore it, and I know that on the basis of that clear voice that night, I and my family moved from Auckland to Perth and we did so with a clear sense that God had called me to be the principal of Vose.

It is one of many reasons why I say that I experience a sense of being 'accompanied' on my journey through life. I really have never felt alone – God never being more than a prayer away.

Let me tell you another story. For me, a little sad. My mother died on 15 May 2012 at the age of 86. In robust good health for most of her life, the end came suddenly after she was diagnosed with a brain tumour. For her it was less than two months between diagnosis and death. I guess because she had been in such good health before, I was stunned. I had always thought she would get to be at least 90, and had a sneaking suspicion she was going to live to be 100. Alas, it was not to be.

I read a portion of the Bible every day. My reading takes two forms: a systematic reading through different books of the Bible, one book at a time, and a more devotional reading from a compilation of Bible verses in a book titled *Living Light*.[7] It gives a different mix of verses around a theme for each day of the year: 366 sets of readings in order to also cover leap years.

I have read from this book almost every day since my wedding (when I was given it) – for more than thirty-seven years at the time of writing. As I turned to the reading that day, 15 May, these were the verses:

> He will wipe every tear from their eyes. There will be no more death or mourning or crying or pain, for the old order of things has passed away.
>
> (Revelation 21:4)

> he will swallow up death for ever. The Sovereign LORD will wipe away the tears from all faces . . .
>
> (Isaiah 25:8)

> your days of sorrow will end . . .
>
> (Isaiah 60:20)

And so it went on. Did it speak to me? Of course it did! Did it reassure me that God knew exactly what had happened and was in control of the process? Naturally.

'That's nice but just a coincidence,' you say. 'The book was bound to look at death sometime, and it just so happened the author selected

15 May, and it's a happy coincidence that is the day your mother died.'

Really?

I can understand why you might say that, because it happened to me, not to you. But because it happened to me, I can't be so quick to dismiss it. At one of my lowest points, I yet again experienced that deep reassurance: 'You are not alone. You are accompanied through life's journey.'

I could continue telling you stories – so many, many of them. And you may or may not believe them. But I believe them, because they happened to me. Put differently, as I have lived my life trusting that God's presence will break through at key periods, I have experienced that this is just what has happened.

I am not claiming that I have never been disappointed or that nothing has ever gone wrong for me. But I am saying, very emphatically, that at the deepest level of my being I believe in God, not simply because my head tells me so (though my head convinces me that there are sound reasons to believe) but because my lived experience provides this as the most convincing explanation. I have chosen to live as though God exists. Having made that choice, I have a narrative that makes sense of the full range of my life experiences. My choice has explanatory power. It does not leave me constantly perplexed and asking endless 'why' questions.

I have been a Christ follower for many decades now, and nothing has caused me to seriously contemplate that God may not exist and that the journey I am on may be misguided. I have worked from the hypothesis that God as revealed in Jesus is real and what Christianity teaches about God and life is so close to accurate that any gap makes no serious difference, and I have found that hypothesis validated in my life experience over and over again. I cannot think of any other explanation of my lived reality that would come even close to holding the different strands of my life together. While this book's title modestly claims to demonstrate why Christianity is probably true, I've moved well beyond the 'probably'. I am not saying I never have fleeting moments of doubt, but when I look back at the full range of my life, doubts evaporate, and I say a little more robustly, 'Jesus is Lord. Christianity is true.'

'Ah,' you may say, 'great to hear your story. But let's talk about the elephant in the room. At an experiential level, Christianity works for you. But we all know of many people who once claimed to be Christians who have now abandoned faith. Yes, marvellous that it's working for you, but clearly there are many for whom it does not work. At best, it seems a little hit-and-miss, and doesn't that seem to indicate that it is largely in the mind?'

There are indeed people who once classified themselves as Christians who have now abandoned faith. The reasons they give are varied. Some have felt let down by God, or may no longer believe that God exists.

Interestingly, a significant study by Alan Jamieson of people who were once very involved in church life, but who no longer attend any church, found that the large majority still claim to have a strong faith and belief in God but are disillusioned with the church.[8] For them, the problem is the church rather than God. And while the church can be a wonderful institution, like all institutions there are times when it can be cold, rigid and unappealing. I have written elsewhere that when we walk into the average church on a Sunday, we quickly recognize that if Jesus were sitting alongside us it is improbable that as the service unfolded he would be nodding in approval and saying to us, 'This is exactly what I had in mind!'[9] In short, the church might well need some significant reforms, but that is no reason to abandon belief in Christianity. In fact, the church has renewed itself many times in the course of history, and there is a strong chance that it will happen again, which could be rather exciting.

While some may be exasperated with institutionalized expressions of faith, for others it is a deeper issue – a genuine crisis of belief. Reasons vary greatly, though a few repeated themes emerge. Some find it impossible to reconcile their understanding of science with Christianity; others are deeply distressed by experiences of Christian hypocrisy or by some of the failures of the church in history; yet others disagree on aspects of the church's teaching. Some have simply found it all too hard.

Jesus himself realized that not all who started the journey of faith would complete it. He told a parable of a sower who was willing to plant seed in different kinds of soils: fertile, rocky, thorny or shallow (Matthew 13:1–23). For most types of soil the expected harvest never resulted, even when there was an initial promising growth.

That explains why some fall from faith – they might not have been ready to take the initial step of trusting God. Jesus put it another way when he suggested that we should not begin the journey of faith unless we first sit down and count the cost (Luke 14:28). He stressed that it was a journey that involved carrying a cross (Matthew 16:24). He wasn't joking. Of his original twelve disciples, Judas Iscariot abandoned him, ten were eventually executed for their faith, and the remaining one, John, was imprisoned on the island of Patmos. Unrealistic expectations can be very damaging, and it is as well to read the Bible carefully, especially focusing on the teaching of Jesus, before any decision to embark on a journey of faith is made.

For all that, there are still instances where sincere and genuine people consciously decide to stop following Jesus. Does this discredit faith, and suggest that the experience of the Christian faith is at best a highly erratic and unreliable pointer towards its validity?

Perhaps we are asking the question the wrong way round. We are asking why some abandon faith. Surely we should ask, 'Why do the vast majority not abandon faith?' After all, every life has its disappointments and setbacks. Following Jesus is often costly, and requires us to put the agenda of Christ, rather than our own, at the centre of our life. Only those who genuinely believe would continue, and the vast majority do.

Seen this way, we quickly face the actual reality. While a relatively small number abandon faith in disappointment, most people who have genuinely embraced faith continue to do so all their life. Clearly I am not talking about those who as children had their parents' faith imposed upon them and as adults have now rejected it. I am talking about those who have seriously and wholeheartedly embraced the Christian faith. Most of them continue with it until their death. Why? Because they have found that day by day, it works. The vast majority would say that it works so well for them that they require no further proof of its validity. If the proof of the pudding is in the eating, this pudding, they would say, is delicious.

Philosopher Nicholas Wolterstorff has written about what he calls 'control beliefs'.[10] These beliefs, adopted in the course of life, exercise control over what can and will be believed. We read life through the lens of these beliefs. The beliefs themselves are usually what we could call 'basic' beliefs – beliefs we no longer need any justification for, because our life works when we hold on to them.

A silly example may make the point. When I wake in the morning, I quickly move to brushing my teeth. It is part of my morning ritual. I don't ask myself, 'Should I clean my teeth this morning?', nor do I agonize over the risks of teeth-cleaning ('What if I brush all my enamel away?') or the cost of toothpaste. I simply clean my teeth and I do so on autopilot. Teeth-cleaning is, for me, a truly basic belief, one which needs no defence or justification.

Could this ever change, so that I no longer clean my teeth automatically? I imagine that if my teeth started to fall out or if some serious mishap resulted from cleaning them, I might reconsider my control belief that teeth-cleaning is a good and necessary thing. But in the absence of any compelling reason for me to re-examine cleaning my teeth, I am unlikely to do so. What I am doing works, and therefore radical review is not called for.

The vast majority of people who have thoughtfully and deliberately put their faith and trust in Jesus operate from the control belief that God is real and known through Jesus. They act upon this belief. They go so far as to build their life upon this belief, and they find that it works.

True, a small number finally decide that it is not for them. But those who have seriously embraced the Christian faith usually stick to it to the very end.

Why?

Because they have found it to be a fully functional and effective control belief. It works, and therefore does not need constant second-guessing.

Perhaps we can therefore end this chapter in the place we started. 'You ask me how I know he lives?' The answer? 'He lives within my heart.' That is the lived experience of literally hundreds and hundreds of millions of people. It may well be your experience. And if not, perhaps it could be, if you are willing to be open to the possibility.

10

Let's Weigh This Up: Why Christianity is Probably True

This book started with some reflections on probability. It set itself the modest task of arguing that Christianity is probably true. It quickly acknowledged that there was unlikely to be a definitive, one-argument-proves-everything case to be made.

This is as it should be. We are called to a life of faith. And faith implies that there is at least a small measure of doubt. For without some doubt, we have certainty, and certainty dismisses faith as surplus to requirements.

A few have been gifted the experience of certainty. The disciples who saw the resurrected Jesus found that all doubt evaporated. Even the most sceptical of them, Thomas, fell on his knees and declared Jesus to be his Lord and God when the resurrected Christ showed him his spear-pierced side and his hands where the nails had been driven through. Perhaps they needed certainty. Each (bar one) was called to follow Jesus at the expense of their own life – a price they willingly paid, because they knew what they had seen and experienced was real. They staked their life upon it without fear.

For us the stakes are unlikely to be as high. Should we decide to follow Jesus, a few might deride us as 'Jesus freaks', but the majority will simply shrug and offer a dismissive 'Whatever'.

Here's a question. What will it take to get you from a point of indifference or scepticism to belief?

If you reply, 'That's not going to happen. I don't believe, and that is simply that', that's pretty closed-minded, don't you think?

Why not sift through the arguments?

You exist. Why? Are you accidentally here, or do you sense that there is some inherent purpose to your life? If the latter, where does this purpose come from? Purpose presupposes a plan, and for there to be a plan, there must have been a planner or a creator.

And what about the sense of 'ought' that most of us have? What sense does it make to suggest that certain things 'ought' to be if this world is essentially accidental?

And what do you make of the world's bestselling book, the Bible? Is it a hoax of astonishing proportions, or a genuinely remarkable text that has helped shape the modern world far more (far, far more) than any other. Its own claim is that it is divinely inspired (2 Timothy 3:16). Is that sheer nonsense, or does the impact it has had clearly demonstrate the reasonableness of the claim? Could a non-inspired text have had anywhere near this influence?

What are we to make of the claim that Jesus was resurrected from the dead? There is little doubt that Jesus' disciples were willing to die rather than retract their statement that he had conquered death. Something about their witness, and the witness of those who followed afterwards, was found to be compelling. It saw the birth of the Christian church. Despite around 260 years of persecution, the church took root in unhospitable soil and grew, and grew, and grew. Today over 2 billion people claim allegiance to this faith that survived against all the odds. Was that luck, or was the hand of God in it?

So many questions to be asked and answered.

We then moved to a more pragmatic test. If God really was involved in the founding of Christianity, surely great good would have come from it. And indeed it has. Name the reform. There are few major societal shifts that have not occurred either directly or indirectly as a result of the Christian faith, be it the value we place on every human life, the abolition of slavery, championing the rights of children and women, the birth of the welfare state, the desire to provide education for all . . . the list goes on and on.

If you doubt this, take a long, hard look at those countries where Christianity has had very little impact. Be honest: are they the places you would like to live, or to raise your children? Probably not. (There's that word 'probably' again!) Whether or not you are a Christian, you are deeply indebted to the Christian faith for helping to birth a kinder, gentler world.

You might be surprised to read these words. You might be more used to hearing Christianity slammed for some of its errors. If you are objective, you will quickly realize that Christianity seems to be judged against a far higher standard than any other faith or philosophy. And that is the unwitting compliment that people consistently pay it. They know how high its standards are. In fact, the church is usually its own strongest critic, having internalized the values of humility and modesty.

But don't be fooled by the bluster against Christianity. A world minus Jesus would have been dramatically the poorer. We rightly date our history against the yardstick of his birth, for his birth was the turning point of all history.

We then turned to the most personal of tests – that of experience. If God is real and actively engaged in the world, surely there would be some evidence of God's existence.

There is an abundance of evidence, provided by hundreds of millions of witnesses, from a wide range of cultures and backgrounds. They have built their life on the belief that God is real and known through Jesus, and they have found that this firm conviction has provided them with a solid foundation for living. Many millions (at least 200 million) go so far as to claim that they have seen God miraculously intervene in their own life, or in the life of others. If this is the act of an 'invisible friend', it appears that 'invisible' is a poor descriptor. So many people can point to tangible things that have happened in their experience. Their emphatic witness is that God's presence with them is anything but invisible. It makes a noticeable and obvious difference.

In the end, evidence has to be weighed, and a verdict given.

I can't make you believe, but I can point you to the reasonableness of faith. In fact, it seems clear to me that Christianity is probably true.

If so, is it unreasonable to suggest that if you have never done so, you take a tentative step towards trusting in God? Pick up a Bible and read its message. Give your local church a chance. If the first is not to your liking, try another. And if you have some Christian friends, why not chat a little more with them and hear how their journey of faith is going.

Do that, and probably before long it will be *your* journey of faith.

Probably . . . why not give it a chance?

Notes

2. So Here's the Problem: Faith is Intellectually Vacuous

[1] Gina A. Bellofatto and Todd M. Johnson, 'Key Findings of *Christianity in Its Global Context, 1970–2020*', *International Bulletin of Missionary Research* 37/3 (2013).

[2] Gabe Bullard, 'The World's Newest Major Religion: No Religion', *National Geographic*, 22 April 2016.

[3] Richard Dawkins, *The God Delusion* (New York, NY: Bantam, 2006).

[4] Dawkins, *God Delusion*, p. 31.

[5] For a fuller evaluation of *The God Delusion*, see Robert Bathurst, 'Debating Dawkins: Confronting the New Atheists' (23 November 2016) http://brianharrisauthor.com/debating-dawkins-confronting-the-new-atheists (accessed 2017).

3. But Have You Considered? Some Logical Reasons to Believe

[1] Theodore Gracyk, 'St. Thomas Aquinas: The Existence of God Can Be Proved in Five Ways' (2016) http://web.mnstate.edu/gracyk/courses/web%20publishing/aquinasFiveWays_ArgumentAnalysis.htm (accessed 2017).

[2] Timothy Keller, *Making Sense of God: An Invitation to the Sceptical* (London: Hodder & Stoughton, 2016), p. 218.

[3] For more on this, written by someone who claims no particular faith, see Paul Davies, *The Goldilocks Enigma: Why the Universe Is Just Right for Life* (London: Penguin Allen Lane, 2006).

[4] Keller, *Making Sense of God*, p. 221.

5   Richard Dawkins, *The Selfish Gene* (Oxford: Oxford University Press, 1976).
6   For more on this, see Vishal Mangalwadi, *The Book That Made Your World: How the Bible Created the Soul of Western Civilization* (Nashville, TN: Thomas Nelson, 2011).
7   Brian Harris, *The Big Picture: Building Blocks of a Christian World View* (Milton Keynes: Paternoster, 2015).
8   Harris, *Big Picture*, pp. 38–9.
9   Dan Brown, *The Da Vinci Code* (New York, NY: Anchor, 2003).
10 Quoted in Lee Strobel, *The Case for Christ: A Journalist's Personal Investigation of the Evidence for Jesus* (Grand Rapids, MI: Zondervan, 1998), p. 78. Strobel's discussion of the issues raised in this section is found in chapter 3 of his book, and is an accessible introduction to what can be a very technical and complex issue.
11 F.F. Bruce, *The Books and the Parchments* (Old Tappan, NJ: Revell, 1963), p. 178.
12 Tertullian, *Apologeticus*, ch. 50, sections 12 and 16.
13 Rodney Stark, *The Rise of Christianity* (Princeton, NJ: Princeton University Press, 1996).
14 Harris, *Big Picture*, p. 55.
15 Bruce L. Shelley, *Church History in Plain Language* (Dallas, TX: Word, 2nd edn, 1995), p. 98.
16 Ambrose, *Letter to Theodosius on the Massacre at Thessalonica* https://www.earlychurchtexts.com/main/ambrose/to_theodosius_on_thessalonica_massacre_01.shtml (accessed 17 Sept. 2019).

5. So Here's the Problem: Faith is Morally Suspect

1   Brian Harris, *When Faith Turns Ugly: Understanding Toxic Faith and How to Avoid It* (Milton Keynes: Paternoster, 2016), pp. xi–xii.
2   Philip Jenkins, *Laying Down the Sword: Why We Can't Ignore the Bible's Violent Verses* (New York, NY: HarperOne, 2011), p. 21.

6. But Have You Considered? Not Such a Shabby History

1   David Kinnaman and Gabe Lyons, *Unchristian: What a New Generation Really Thinks about Christianity . . . and Why It Matters* (Grand Rapids, MI: Baker, 2007).

2   Alvin J. Schmidt, *Under the Influence: How Christianity Transformed Culture* (Grand Rapids, MI: Zondervan, 2001).
3   Vishal Mangalwadi, *The Book That Made Your World: How the Bible Created the Soul of Western Civilization* (Nashville, TN: Thomas Nelson, 2011), p. 302.
4   Cited in Schmidt, *Under the Influence*, p. 49.
5   Schmidt, *Under the Influence*, p. 74.
6   Plautus, *Trinummus* 2:338–9; cited in Schmidt, *Under the Influence*, p. 129.
7   Schmidt, *Under the Influence*, p. 131.
8   Cited in Schmidt, *Under the Influence*, p. 153.
9   Cited in Schmidt, *Under the Influence*, p. 172.
10 The story of Hannah More makes especially fascinating reading in this regard. Karen Swallow Prior, *Fierce Convictions: The Extraordinary Life of Hannah More – Poet, Reformer, Abolitionist* (Nashville, TN: Nelson Books, 2014).
11 See Greg Sheridan, *God Is Good for You: A Defence of Christianity in Troubled Times* (Sydney: Allen & Unwin, 2018), pp. 96–123.

7. Let's Weigh This Up

1   Malia Martin's estimate is of between 85 and 100 million. Malia Martin, 'Foreword', in *The Black Book of Communism: Crimes, Terror, Repression* (ed. Stéphane Courtois and Mark Kramer; Cambridge, MA: Harvard University Press, 1999), p. xi.

9. But Have You Considered? The Witness of Faith from the Inside

1   From the hymn 'He Lives' (Ackley); in public domain.
2   Francis Spufford, *Unapologetic: Why, Despite Everything, Christianity Can Still Make Surprising Emotional Sense* (London: Faber & Faber, 2012), p. 19.
3   I'm indebted to Philip Yancey's book *Disappointment with God* for sparking many of the ideas in this section. Philip Yancey, *Disappointment with God: Three Questions No One Asks Aloud* (Grand Rapids, MI: Zondervan, 1988).

⁴ Harold S. Kushner, *When Bad Things Happen to Good People* (New York, NY: Anchor, 2004).

⁵ Yancey, *Disappointment with God*. The story of Duncan is told in ch. 24, 'Is God Unfair?'.

⁶ Craig S. Keener, *Miracles: The Credibility of the New Testament Accounts* (2 vols; Grand Rapids, MI: Baker, 2011).

⁷ Edythe Draper, *Living Light: Daily Light in Today's Language* (Wheaton, IL: Tyndale House, 1972).

⁸ Alan Jamieson, *A Churchless Faith: Faith Journeys beyond Evangelical, Pentecostal and Charismatic Churches* (Wellington: Philip Garside, 2000).

⁹ Brian Harris, *The Big Picture: Building Blocks of a Christian World View* (Milton Keynes: Paternoster, 2015), p. xv.

¹⁰ Nicholas Wolterstorff, *Reason within the Bounds of Religion* (Grand Rapids, MI: Eerdmans, 1976).

References

Bathurst, Robert. 'Debating Dawkins: Confronting the New Atheists' (23 November 2016) http://brianharrisauthor.com/debating-dawkins-confronting-the-new-atheists/ (accessed 2017).

Bellofatto, Gina A., and Todd M. Johnson. 'Key Findings of *Christianity in Its Global Context, 1970–2020*'. *International Bulletin of Missionary Research* 37/3 (2013): pp. 164.

Brown, Dan. *The Da Vinci Code* (New York, NY: Anchor, 2003).

Bruce, F.F. *The Books and the Parchments* (Old Tappan, NJ: Revell, 1963).

Bullard, Gabe. 'The World's Newest Major Religion: No Religion'. *National Geographic*, 22 April 2016.

Davies, Paul. *The Goldilocks Enigma: Why the Universe Is Just Right for Life* (London: Penguin Allen Lane, 2006).

Dawkins, Richard. *The God Delusion* (New York, NY: Bantam, 2006).

———. *The Selfish Gene* (Oxford: Oxford University Press, 1976).

Draper, Edythe. *Living Light: Daily Light in Today's Language* (Wheaton, IL: Tyndale House, 1972).

Gracyk, Theodore. 'St. Thomas Aquinas: The Existence of God Can Be Proved in Five Ways' (2016) http://web.mnstate.edu/gracyk/courses/web%20publishing/aquinasFiveWays_ArgumentAnalysis.htm (accessed 2017).

Harris, Brian. *The Big Picture: Building Blocks of a Christian World View* (Milton Keynes: Paternoster, 2015).

———. *When Faith Turns Ugly: Understanding Toxic Faith and How to Avoid It* (Milton Keynes: Paternoster, 2016).

Jamieson, Alan. *A Churchless Faith: Faith Journeys beyond Evangelical, Pentecostal and Charismatic Churches* (Wellington: Philip Garside, 2000).

Jenkins, Philip. *Laying Down the Sword: Why We Can't Ignore the Bible's Violent Verses* (New York, NY: HarperOne, 2011).

Keener, Craig S. *Miracles: The Credibility of the New Testament Accounts* (2 vols; Grand Rapids, MI: Baker, 2011).

Keller, Timothy. *Making Sense of God: An Invitation to the Sceptical* (London: Hodder & Stoughton, 2016).

Kinnaman, David and Gabe Lyons. *Unchristian: What a New Generation Really Thinks about Christianity . . . and Why It Matters* (Grand Rapids, MI: Baker, 2007).

Kushner, Harold S. *When Bad Things Happen to Good People* (New York, NY: Anchor, 2004).

Mangalwadi, Vishal. *The Book That Made Your World: How the Bible Created the Soul of Western Civilization* (Nashville, TN: Thomas Nelson, 2011).

Martin, Malia. 'Foreword.' In *The Black Book of Communism: Crimes, Terror, Repression* (ed. Stephane Courtois and Mark Kramer; Cambridge, MA: Harvard University Press, 1999).

Prior, Karen Swallow. *Fierce Convictions: The Extraordinary Life of Hannah More – Poet, Reformer, Abolitionist* (Nashville, TN: Nelson Books, 2014).

Schmidt, Alvin J. *Under the Influence: How Christianity Transformed Culture* (Grand Rapids, MI: Zondervan, 2001).

Shelley, Bruce L. *Church History in Plain Language* (Dallas, TX: Word, 2nd edn, 1995).

Sheridan, Greg. *God Is Good for You: A Defence of Christianity in Troubled Times* (Sydney: Allen & Unwin, 2018).

Spufford, Francis. *Unapologetic: Why, Despite Everything, Christianity Can Still Make Surprising Emotional Sense* (London: Faber & Faber, 2012).

Stark, Rodney. *The Rise of Christianity* (Princeton, NJ: Princeton University Press, 1996).

Strobel, Lee. *The Case for Christ: A Journalist's Personal Investigation of the Evidence for Jesus* (Grand Rapids, MI: Zondervan, 1998).

Wolterstorff, Nicholas. *Reason within the Bounds of Religion* (Grand Rapids, MI: Eerdmans, 1976).

Yancey, Philip. *Disappointment with God: Three Questions No One Asks Aloud* (Grand Rapids, MI: Zondervan, 1988).

The Big Picture

*Building Blocks of a
Christian World View*

Brian Harris

The Big Picture is an accessible and stimulating exploration of
the big building blocks of the Christian faith. Harris's take
on the big building blocks of Christian faith is refreshing and
will be appreciated by all who would like to think through
different ways to follow Jesus the Christ in an ever-changing
context.

'Skilfully bringing together biblically-informed theology and the
everyday world, Brian Harris unpacks themes of grace, creation
and Christian hope in an engaging conversational manner.
The result is a book that empowers us to live out our faith
wherever we are.' – *Stephen Garner, Laidlaw College, Auckland,
New Zealand*

978-1-84227-856-7

**Evidence That Demands
a Verdict**

*Life-changing truth for a
sceptical world
(Anglicized edition)*

*Josh McDowell & Sean
McDowell, PhD*

For more than 40 years, *Evidence That Demands a Verdict* has
encouraged and strengthened millions of people around the
world.

Evidence is now thoroughly revised and updated from previous
editions in light of newly uncovered historical documentation
and the best of modern scholarship. That means you'll gain new
insights to growth in your faith and be better equipped to answer
the questions and objections of today's most hardened sceptics.

Evidence brings you all-new and expanded chapters to challenge
the latest attacks from Christianity's critics. No matter the
topic – evidence for the Bible's authenticity, evidence for the
historical Jesus and his resurrection, evidence for the accuracy of
the Old Testament, or evidence for the truth claims of the
Bible – this new edition is the go-to source for fast, accurate
answers.

978-1-78078-832-6

When Rain Falls Like Lead

Exploring the Presence of God in the Darkness of Suffering

Andrew Percey

'Why does God allow suffering?' 'Where is God in my suffering?'

These are the big questions that we all grapple with at some point in our lives. This unique, biblically-rooted and pastorally-focused book explores these questions in a sensitive and compelling way. Finding himself wrestling with these questions when his sister died suddenly, Percey delivers an honest, personal and poignant look at the issues. Whilst never shying away from the pain and reality of suffering, this book weaves together biblical truths with genuine hope to help us see that God really is present, even in the darkness.

Andrew Percey is the minister of Manvers Street Baptist Church, Bath

978-1-84227-813-0

Towards Belief DVD

Karl Faase

Is it reasonable to be a person of faith? How can we deal with issues of suffering, science, violence, abuse and the supernatural in our consideration of God? *Towards Belief* is a 10-part DVD series that sets out to defuse the belief blockers of our time and is an essential resource for all churches and ministry groups committed to helping people explore Christian faith.

Contributors include John Lennox, Amy Orr-Ewing, Nicky Gumbel and John Dickson. *Towards Belief* comes complete with two DVDs and a Discussion Guide for personal or group study.

978-0-98062-668-1

Paternoster:
thinking faith

We trust you enjoyed reading this book
from Paternoster. If you want to be
informed of any new titles from this
author and other releases you can sign
up to the Paternoster newsletter by
scanning below:

Online:
authenticmedia.co.uk/paternoster

Follow us: